# UNKNOWN
## CHICAGO TALES

# UNKNOWN
## CHICAGO TALES

JOHN R. SCHMIDT

THE
History
PRESS

Published by The History Press
Charleston, SC
www.historypress.com

*Front cover*: (*Top, middle*) A view of Chicago from the upper deck of Wrigley Field. *Photograph taken by the author.*

First published 2021

Manufactured in the United States

ISBN 9781467147521

Library of Congress Control Number: 2020951994

# CONTENTS

Acknowledgements                                    9
Introduction                                       11

1. CHICAGO BF (BEFORE THE FIRE)
    Father of Chicago                              13
    Billy Caldwell the Man                         15
    A Slave in Chicago                             17
    A Murder Most Foul                             19
    The Celebrity                                  21
    Opera House Lottery                            23

2. BUILDERS AND CHARACTERS
    Chicago's Saint                                26
    The Life and Death of Nails Morton             28
    Mighty Milton Sills                            30
    The Aviator                                    32
    One-Eye Connelly                               35
    Architect of the Good Life                     37
    The Constant Candidate                         39
    Miss Frances                                   41
    Mile-A-Minute Harry                            43
    Joseph Medill's Last Words                     45

# CONTENTS

3. POLITICS AND POLITICOS
Who Was Dan Ryan?   48
Blond Boss Billy   50
The Rosemont Corridor   52
The First Cullerton   54
Why the Kennedy Curves at Division Street   56
Starring Martin Kennelly   58
The Sullivan of Sullivan High School   61
A Tale of Two Kellys   63
A Tale of Two Tombs   65
Bathhouse John   67

4. SPORTS AND SPORTSMEN
Cap Anson   70
Man of Steel   72
Chicago's Forgotten Baseball Team   74
A Winning Chicago Athlete   76
Bowler of the Half-Century   77
Chicago's Forgotten Football Team   80
Godfather of Big-Bucks Golf   82
Going Stagg   84
Chicago's Forgotten Basketball Teams   86

5. THE CHICAGO WAY
Where Have You Gone, Terrible Tommy?   89
Gross Cyrano   91
A Different Saint Valentine's Day Story   93
An Editor's Scoop   95
The Short, Unhappy Life of Algren Street   97
The Bowling Ball That Went Around the World   100
Bertillonage in Chicago   102
Waiters' Revenge?   104
Sic Transit Gloria Hinky Dink   107

6. FORGOTTEN CHICAGO MOVIES
*In Old Chicago* (1937)   110
*City That Never Sleeps* (1953)   112
*Al Capone* (1959)   114
*Gaily, Gaily* (1969)   115

# CONTENTS

*Cooley High* (1975)                                                117
*Continental Divide* (1981)                                        119

7. THE PASSING PARADE
Professor Moriarty Comes to Chicago                      122
Kiss of Fire                                                          124
The Original Walking Man                                     126
The Other Chicago Fire                                         128
The Annie Oakley Cocaine Case                             130
Judy's Jolly Jaunt                                               132
The Chicago Grand Prix of 1895                           134
Death Valley Scotty's Wild Ride                            136
World's Parliament of Religions                            138

About the Author                                                 141

# ACKNOWLEDGEMENTS

Most of my research was carried out at the Regenstein Library of the University of Chicago, as well as at the Harold Washington Library in downtown Chicago. My thanks go to the staffs of both places, particularly to Betsy Vera and Michelle Sudeikis at the Harold Washington Library. For their ongoing support and encouragement, thank you also to Keith Hamilton and Mike Panozzo of *Bowlers Journal*, and to Chicago radio legend Justin Kaufmann. And a giant thank you to Ben Gibson and Ashley Hill of The History Press for guiding this book through to publication.

My children, Nick Schmidt and Tracy Samantha Goodheart, have long since moved out on their own and no longer have to listen to my history stories, but I thank them for their continuing feedback. My wife, Terri Schmidt, still lives with me, still shows remarkable patience with me and still offers wise and loving advice on all aspects of my work. I dedicate this book to her—not because I'm supposed to but because she deserves it.

—A.M.D.G.

# INTRODUCTION

The title *Unknown Chicago Tales* sums up this book. It's the history you didn't learn. These are the stories that other books skip. They are the spices that enhance the city's distinctive flavor. This is a collection of short, seven-hundred-word sketches. The setting is Chicagoland—not just the city proper but also the suburbs and the exurbs. The content is eclectic.

Here are people—builders and bounders, politicians and sportsmen and more than a few eccentrics. Here are tales that will raise a chuckle or cause a groan. Here are some of the lesser-known classic movies that every Chicagoan should see. This book will talk about forgotten celebrities, such as the early-day children's TV star who set the standard for Mr. Rogers or the pioneer aviator who overcame the twin obstacles of being a woman and being black. This book will visit the man who founded a 150-year-long Chicago political dynasty. This book will remember the swimmer who never lost a competitive race and the dignified newspaper editor who published the most outrageous example of "fake news" in the annals of journalism.

Did you know that Chicago's long-celebrated Mr. Pioneer Settler went to court so he could keep a slave? Did you know that Sherlock Holmes's nemesis Professor Moriarty was a real person who pulled off a caper in Chicago? What do you know about the Second Chicago Fire, which took place three years after the famous one? And why did the county jail save its gallows for fifty years?

Welcome to *Unknown Chicago Tales*—because Chicago history is about more than just a fire.

# 1.

# CHICAGO BF (BEFORE THE FIRE)

## FATHER OF CHICAGO

"The first White man to settle in Chicago was Black." This was a popular witticism around town in the 1930s, and it says much about the attitudes of the time. Of course, the person referred to is Jean Baptiste Pointe DuSable.

DuSable was the first nonindigenous settler in the area that became Chicago. We know that. But much of the historical record is fuzzy. Even his name has different versions, such as "au Sable" or "de Saible." We also have no real idea of his physical appearance, except that he was a big man. Any DuSable biography is speculative. The story that follows is drawn from a number of different sources, some of them contradictory.

He was born in Santa Domingo (modern Haiti) around 1745. His father was a French mariner—some stories say a pirate—and his mother was an enslaved African. According to legend, when Jean Baptiste's mother was killed during a Spanish raid, the boy swam out to his father's ship to take refuge. After that, the older DuSable took his son to France to be educated.

Along with a friend, Jean Baptiste arrived in New Orleans in 1764. The two young men became traders, journeying up the Mississippi River and through the Midwest as far as present-day Michigan. During this time, DuSable married a Potawatomi woman and became a member of the tribe. The Potawatomi called him Black Chief.

Sometime after 1770, DuSable moved to the region known as Eschecagou, which visitors mispronounced as "Chicago." He built a fur trading post at the mouth of the local river, near where the Tribune Tower now stands. It's also said that he operated a distillery on the site. Besides French, he spoke English, Spanish, and several Native dialects.

Then came the American Revolution. Though DuSable's trading post was far away from the war's main theater, he was a French national with Potawatomi connections. The British were suspicious of him. In 1779 he was arrested and taken to Fort Mackinac. There DuSable somehow worked out a deal with his captors to manage a British trading post on the St. Clair River.

DuSable reclaimed his Chicago property after the war ended in 1783. Besides his twenty-two-by-forty-foot log cabin residence, he built two barns, a mill, a bakery, a dairy, a workshop, a henhouse, and a smokehouse. He was now selling pork, bread, and flour. As an adopted Potawatomi, he enjoyed good relations with the Native peoples. Many of them worked for him.

In 1800 DuSable abruptly sold his holdings. Why he did this is a mystery. One story claims that he had unsuccessfully tried to become the chief of a local Potawatomi band. Another source said that he was growing older and had become weary of managing his various businesses—he wanted a simpler life. He farmed a small piece of land near Peoria for about ten years until his wife died. Then he moved in with his granddaughter in St. Charles, Missouri.

He had once been spoken of as a wealthy man, but most of that wealth was gone then. Jean Baptiste Pointe DuSable died at his granddaughter's house on August 28, 1818, and was buried in the local Catholic cemetery. His grave site remained unmarked until 1968.

After DuSable left Chicago, his property on the riverbank eventually passed on to John Kinzie. As the years went by, Kinzie was hailed as Mr. Pioneer Settler. DuSable was forgotten.

The city's first recognition of DuSable came in 1912, when a plaque was placed on a building near his cabin site. During the 1930s the board of education opened DuSable High School at 4934 South Wabash Avenue in the city's African American neighborhood. Some Chicago street guides from that era list DeSaible Square at 3728 south, between 500 and 551 east.

In more recent times, DuSable has been honored in many ways. The DuSable Museum of African American History was established in Washington Park, and the postal service issued a DuSable stamp as part of its Black Heritage series. In 2006, the Chicago City Council officially recognized him as the founder of Chicago.

Jean Baptiste Pointe DuSable surveys the site of his homestead. *Photograph by the author.*

The latest memorial to Jean Baptiste Pointe DuSable is an outdoor statuary bust. Dedicated in 2009, it's located on Michigan Avenue, just north of the river—right near his old front door.

## BILLY CALDWELL THE MAN

People on the far Northwest Side of Chicago, around Cicero and Peterson Avenues, know the name Billy Caldwell. There is Billy Caldwell Woods, Billy Caldwell's Reserve, the Billy Caldwell Golf Course, the Billy Caldwell Post of the American Legion. And, of course, there is Caldwell Avenue.

The neighborhood is called Sauganash. That was Billy Caldwell's other name.

William Caldwell Jr. was born near Fort Niagara, in upstate New York, in 1782. He was the biological son of a British army captain and a Mohawk woman. There is some evidence that Billy's first name was actually Thomas. When Captain Caldwell was transferred to another post, he abandoned his infant son to be raised by the Mohawks.

Sometime around 1789, the elder Caldwell sent for Billy. The captain had settled near Detroit, married an English woman, and started raising a family. Billy received a basic education and worked the family farm. The boy didn't

15

have much standing in the White society of the day—he was both a bastard and a "half-breed." At seventeen he moved out on his own.

Billy apprenticed himself into the fur trade. By 1803 he was head clerk in the Kinzie-Forsyth firm's post at the mouth of the Chicago River. Around this time he married into the Potawatomi tribe. His in-laws called him *Sauganash*, which loosely translates as "Englishman."

In 1812 the Potawatomi attacked the American garrison at Fort Dearborn. The story goes that Caldwell arrived on the scene just after the battle and saved the lives of the Kinzie family. Historians have been unable to determine what actually happened.

The Battle of Fort Dearborn was one of the first skirmishes in the War of 1812. Caldwell considered himself a loyal Briton, like his father, and fought on the British side in the war. He also helped recruit Native tribes as allies. Some sources claim that he served as an advisor to the great Shawnee warrior-chief Tecumseh.

Caldwell lived in Canada after the war ended in 1815. He worked for a time in the colony's Indian Department. Then he tried several business ventures, all of which failed. By 1820 he was back in Chicago.

The Native tribes had fought in the war to stop American expansion into their lands. Once the fighting ended, the British made no effort help them. For Caldwell, it was another in a series of disappointments he'd suffered from his father's people. He decided to throw in with the Americans.

In Chicago, Caldwell was once again active in the Native trade. He also worked as an appraiser. Because of his tribal connections and his fluency in several languages, Caldwell smoothed relations between the Americans and the Native peoples. He made friends among the settlement's leaders, became an American citizen, and held a number of minor political posts.

The U.S. government recognized Caldwell's work by building Chicago's first frame house for him, near where Holy Name Cathedral now stands. This is yet another legend that has not been documented. But in 1829 he was appointed chief of the Potawatomi. And that needs explaining.

The Potawatomi knew that the Americans were trying to force them out. They wanted to get the best deal possible. Although Caldwell was Mohawk—and only on his mother's side—the Potawatomi thought he could help them in treaty negotiations. So, they accepted him as chief.

The Potawatomi then started signing off their land. Caldwell became a hero among the American settlers. Chicago's first hotel was named The Sauganash in his honor. The U.S. government awarded him a 1,600-acre tract of land northwest of the city, Billy Caldwell's Reserve.

Welcome to Sauganash, Mr. Caldwell's neighborhood. *Photograph by the author.*

With the 1833 Treaty of Chicago, the Potawatomi gave up the last of their land. At fifty-one, Caldwell was an old man for the time. Now that the native peoples were leaving, there was no need for his services and no reason for him to stay in Chicago. He sold his reserve and left with his adopted tribe.

He'd lived a life on the margins, bouncing around among at least three different worlds, never fully a part of any of them. Billy Caldwell spent his final years with the Potawatomi near Council Bluffs, Iowa. He died there in 1841.

# A SLAVE IN CHICAGO

*Twelve Years a Slave* won the Academy Award for Best Picture a few years ago. The film was based on the memoir of Solomon Northup, a free Black man who was kidnapped and sold into slavery during the 1840s. Four decades before Northup's ordeal, something similar happened in Chicago.

In 1804 John Kinzie moved into the old DuSable cabin on the north bank of the Chicago River and began trading with the Native tribes. Thomas

Forsyth Jr., his half-brother, was in business with him. That spring, the partners took on an indentured servant named Jeffrey Nash.

His indenture papers describe Nash as a "Negro man." According to that contract, he was to serve Kinzie and Forsyth for a period of seven years. For their part, the two traders were to provide him with "meat, drink, apparel, washing, and lodging fitting for a servant."

In return for these benefits, Nash bound himself to faithfully obey the commands of his "masters." He would do no damage to them or their goods, and would keep their secrets. He would be on call, day and night, for whenever his service was needed.

Nash agreed to a personal code of conduct as well. During the seven years of his indenture, he agreed that he would not play cards or dice. He would not frequent taverns without permission from Kinzie or Forsyth. He also pledged that he would not "commit fornication nor contract matrimony."

On May 22, 1804, Nash put his mark to the indenture. Since Illinois was not yet a state, the papers were sent to the territorial capital in Detroit.

Kinzie and Forsyth operated a second trading post in Peoria. That was Forsyth's principal residence. Sometime after the 1804 indenture was instituted, Forsyth took Nash there. And sometime later, Nash ran away. He eventually made his way to New Orleans, where he got married and started a family.

The traders were not about to just let Nash go. In 1813, they began proceedings in Louisiana to get him back. The case was labeled *Kensy* [sic] *and Forsyth, plaintiffs v. Jeffrey Nash, defendant.*

Now the plaintiffs claimed that Nash was not a free-born servant under indenture but was actually their slave. Residents of Peoria had recognized Nash as Forsyth's slave. Nash himself was said to have admitted being a slave and had run away when Forsyth broke a promise to free him. The traders also produced a bill of sale, dated September 5, 1803, that transferred the ownership of Nash to them.

Looking at the case many years later, some historians have concluded that the 1803 bill of sale must have been a forgery. If Nash had already been their slave, why would Kinzie and Forsyth go to the trouble of having him put his mark on an indenture document?

Other historians don't buy this argument. They reason that the indenture document was a type of insurance policy for Kinzie and Forsyth. In 1804, with new territories being organized, the partners were not sure they'd be allowed to keep Nash as a slave. If he were an indentured servant, they could hold onto him for seven years. Later, when Nash escaped to Louisiana, they dug up the 1803 slave bill of sale. Since Louisiana was a slave state, the partners were confident they'd be able to reclaim Nash.

In 1816 the case was decided by the Supreme Court of Louisiana. Judge Francis Xavier Martin rendered the decision. He accepted the September 5, 1803 bill of sale as legitimate. Kinzie and Forsyth had indeed purchased Jeffrey Nash as a slave.

Now for the big "however."

However, the Northwest Ordinance of 1787 banned slavery from the territory that would eventually become Ohio, Indiana, Michigan, Illinois, and Wisconsin. The only exceptions were for persons convicted of a crime or fugitive slaves escaping a slave-holding state. Nash did not fall under either of these categories. Therefore, the court ruled in his favor. He would remain a free man.

"Thus did the Supreme Court of the slave state of Louisiana uphold the free character of the soil of Illinois and rescue a man from bondage," historian Milo Milton Quaife later wrote. As for Kinzie and Forsyth, they had to pay the court costs.

# A MURDER MOST FOUL

It all began with some stray cows.

In 1840 Lucretia Thompson was a young woman who lived with her husband on a farm about ten miles up the north branch of the Chicago River in an area known as Big Woods. On the morning of April 4, she set out to look for her missing cows. Later that day, a neighbor found the cows and brought them back to the farm. But Mrs. Thompson did not return.

That was Saturday. On Sunday, the local men formed a search party. They continued searching through Monday and into Tuesday. Finally, on Tuesday evening, one of the searchers noticed a bunch of hogs gathered in a spot about a half-mile from the Thompson farm. When he shooed the hogs away, he discovered the half-eaten body of Lucretia Thompson.

Her skull had been smashed. A club covered with hair and pieces of brain matter was found near the body, as was part of a red shirt sleeve. The woman appeared to have been running toward her home when someone caught her, overcame her struggles, and killed her.

Suspicion soon fell on John Stone. A thirty-four-year-old Irishman, he had been out chopping wood when Mrs. Thompson disappeared. Later he was

Big Woods, a Cook County forest preserve, today. *Photograph by the author.*

seen burning his shirt and pants. He said they had become infected with lice. When he was examined, it was found that he had bruises on his arm.

Stone was placed under arrest. On the way into the city, he asked the guard for his opinions about the case. He particularly wanted to know if a man could be hanged for murder if there were no witnesses.

On May 1, the trial of John Stone for the murder of Lucretia Thompson opened. Stone pleaded not guilty. The case against him was circumstantial. In evidence, there was the piece of torn shirt sleeve, the bruises on Stone's arm, and a footprint near the victim that seemed to match Stone's boot. There was also the uncorroborated testimony of one man, who said Stone had bragged that he would "have intercourse" with Mrs. Thompson.

The jury got the case on May 4. Three days later, they told the judge they were deadlocked. They asked that certain witnesses be recalled. After hearing further testimony, the jurors retired to their chamber. A few minutes later, they came back with a guilty verdict. The judge set Stone's execution for May 29.

Stone's lawyers immediately appealed the verdict, petitioning the Illinois Supreme Court for a new trial. The execution was delayed while the court considered the petition. In due course, the justices denied the appeal. Stone was then scheduled to be hanged on July 10.

Newspapers in other cities had reprinted accounts of Lucretia Thompson's murder. The story was even carried in the Irish press, presumably because John Stone was Irish. In the days before the hanging, new details about Stone's background were released. It was said he had been part of group that burned an American ship, had served time for rape in New York State, had been under a death sentence in Canada and escaped, had already killed several men. None of these tales were ever proven.

With Stone's appeals exhausted, Chicago geared up for its first hanging. In 1834 a laborer had gone to trial for killing his wife but was acquitted. In 1835 a drifter accused of murder had his trial shifted to Iroquois County, and wound up being hanged there. Now Chicago would have its turn!

At noon on July 10, Stone was escorted out of the log cabin court lockup and placed in a wagon to begin his last journey. Gallows had been constructed behind Myrick's Tavern, near what is now Twenty-Ninth Street and King Drive. Escorting the prisoner was a squad of sixty militiamen, as well as two hundred armed volunteers on horseback.

Around three thousand people had gathered to watch the spectacle. After a short Episcopalian service, Stone addressed the crowd. He reasserted his innocence. He said that two people had killed Mrs. Thompson. He knew who they were but would "rather swing" than identify them.

With that, a hood was placed over John Stone's head, and he was hanged by the neck until he was dead. His corpse was then given over to a physician for dissection.

# THE CELEBRITY

If you've read *Huckleberry Finn*, you know about the King and the Duke. They are the two con men who latch onto Huck and Jim, claiming to be European nobility.

Around the same time that Huck and his companions were going down the Mississippi, the young city of Chicago had its own, real-life version of the King and the Duke. His name was David Kennison. He said he was the last survivor of the Boston Tea Party.

David Kennison spelled his name various ways—"Kinniston" is just one of the other variations. He came to Chicago as an old man around 1848, living on a small pension as a veteran of the War of 1812. He took lodging with the William Mack family on the West Side. Then he began telling his stories.

David Kennison, the last survivor of the Boston Tea Party—maybe. *From the* Chicago Tribune, *February 24, 1901.*

Kennison said that he had been born in New Hampshire in 1736. He grew up in Maine, and by 1773, he was active in patriotic resistance to British taxation. On December 16 of that year, he was in the party that boarded the merchant ship in Boston Harbor and threw the crates of tea overboard.

But the Tea Party was only the beginning of Kennison's exploits. He managed to find himself present at most of the important events of the American Revolution. He was at the battles of Bunker Hill, White Plains, and Brandywine, along with other skirmishes. For a time, he was a dispatch runner for General Washington, which put him at West Point when Benedict Arnold's treachery was discovered. Kennison was captured by the Mohawks, was held prisoner for seventeen months, then escaped. And he was there at Yorktown in 1781, when Cornwallis surrendered.

Somehow, Kennison had missed the signing of the Declaration of Independence. Still, he had done his part in winning that independence, and he retired from warfare to take up farming—until those nasty Brits provoked the War of 1812. So once again, he took up his musket. He had gone through the Revolution without a scratch, but now he suffered a hand wound from some grapeshot. Obviously, his reflexes were slowing down.

When the war ended, Kennison went back to farming. And marrying a succession of four wives. And fathering twenty-two children.

So spoke David Kennison. Now Chicago welcomed him with great joy. For a growing frontier town, it was quite an honor to have such a distinguished person as a resident. Kennison was given free food, free drinks, free clothes, and free rent. He repaid the generosity with other stirring stories of his adventures.

Kennison also used his celebrity status to make an endorsement in the 1848 presidential election. He declared that he had always opposed slavery. But rather than waste a vote on Martin Van Buren's Free Soil Party, Kennison intended to vote for regular Democrat Lewis Cass and urged all like-minded Chicagoans to do the same. Zachary Taylor of the Whigs won the election anyway.

Finally, as it must to everyone, death came to David Kennison on February 24, 1852, at the reported age of 115. His funeral the next day was the most spectacular Chicago had yet seen.

Afternoon services were conducted at the Clark Street Methodist Church. Then the cortege moved off through the North Side. The hearse was accompanied by an army detachment, several companies of militia, volunteer firemen, and a military band. The mayor and city council followed in carriages. Most of the city's forty thousand people lined the streets. David Kennison was laid to rest in City Cemetery with full military honors. Then Chicago went back to work.

Years later, City Cemetery became Lincoln Park. The bodies were removed and reburied elsewhere. In the meantime, Kennison's grave had been lost. A marker was eventually placed at a probable location, near Clark and Wisconsin Streets.

Today most historians discount David Kennison's Revolution stories. The consensus is that he was probably a veteran of the War of 1812 and that he was merely in his eighties when he died.

And yet…

Presumably, Kennison's remains are still somewhere in Lincoln Park. And if they are ever found, scientific testing can determine whether he was really 115 years old when he died. And while that wouldn't prove that he had taken part in the Boston Tea Party, it might earn him a statue.

# OPERA HOUSE LOTTERY

Uranus Crosby thought big. Perhaps it came from being named after a planet. Today we remember him for giving Chicago one of its grandest buildings—and one of its shadiest deals.

Crosby arrived in Chicago from Massachusetts in the 1850s. Along with a cousin, he went into the liquor distilling business and prospered. Then came the Civil War. According to one story, Crosby guessed that the federal government would finance the war by raising the excise tax, so he produced and purchased all the spirits he could. When the tax did go up, he undercut his competitors and made a fortune.

By the end of 1864, the war was winding down. Crosby had become one of Chicago's most prominent citizens. Compared to dear old New England, his adopted city was a cultural wasteland. He decided that Chicago needed a suitable venue dedicated to grand opera and began building one.

Crosby's Opera House on Lottery Day. *Author's collection.*

Located on Washington Street, west of State Street, Crosby's Opera House cost $700,000 to construct. Its grand opening was set for April 17, 1865, but was delayed for three days because of President Lincoln's assassination. When the performances finally got going, business was slow. Crosby had evidently misread the city's desire for the finer things.

Crosby was broke but not discouraged. He came up with a novel plan to recoup his losses. He would give away his opera house and its artwork in a lottery.

The Crosby Opera House Art Association was formed to conduct the lottery. Rather than think they were gambling, patrons were encouraged to believe they were promoting culture. For a five-dollar donation, patrons received an engraving of a famous painting. Almost as an afterthought, a lottery ticket and an illustrated catalogue of prizes went along with the engraving.

The drawing was scheduled for October 11, 1866. Then Crosby announced it would be delayed for three months. He said the demand for tickets made him extend the deadline. More likely, he simply hadn't sold enough.

The new drawing was to take place on January 21, 1867. In the meantime, the public was invited to visit the opera house to examine the treasures they might soon possess. Crosby finally sold a total of 210,000 tickets.

On the morning of January 21, special trains brought ticket buyers into the city for the big event. The crowd spilled out of the opera house itself and onto the street. Extra police were on hand to keep order.

Crosby had enlisted a coterie of distinguished people to perform the drawing. At precisely 11:00 a.m., the first ticket number was pulled out of a drum on stage. A prize ticket was then pulled out of a second drum and the two were matched. This went on until 112 pieces of art had been awarded.

Then it was time for the big prize—the opera house itself. Ticket #58,600 was pulled, but the winner was not present. The drawing then resumed until all the other prizes were accounted for.

*Who had won the grand prize?* The *Tribune* wondered whether the whole thing had been a swindle. But by the next day, the winner had been identified as A.H. Lee of Prairie du Rocher, Illinois.

Everyone was eager to get a look at this lucky fellow. When contacted, Lee said his wife was sick and that he couldn't make the trip to Chicago. A few days later, Crosby made another announcement. It seemed Lee was shy and didn't want the publicity. He had come into Chicago secretly and received the deed to the opera house. Then Lee had sold it back to Crosby for $200,000.

The public had bought over $1,000,000 in chances on a $700,000 building. Subtracting the $200,000 given to Lee, Crosby had paid off the construction costs, pocketed a $100,000 profit, and still had the opera house. And of course, there were questions about whether A.H. Lee even existed. Anticipating that the disgruntled villagers of Chicago might soon be coming after him with torches and pitchforks, Uranus Crosby left the city and went back to Massachusetts.

An uncle took over managing the Crosby properties. In 1868 the opera house hosted the Republican National Convention, which launched Ulysses S. Grant on the road to the presidency. Three years later, the fabled building was destroyed in the Great Fire.

# 2

# BUILDERS AND CHARACTERS

## CHICAGO'S SAINT

It's a story they told in the newsroom of the *Chicago American* many years ago.

A young reporter named Harry Reutlinger had been sent to get an interview with a patient at Columbus Hospital. The patient was involved in a criminal case, and the police were keeping a tight lid on him.

At the hospital, Reutlinger encountered a little old woman mopping floors. "Don't worry. I'm supposed to be here," he told her. "Mother Cabrini sent for me." Frances Xavier Cabrini was the famous nun who ran the hospital.

The cleaning lady wasn't buying that. So, Reutlinger snuck around the side of the building and came in through a fire escape. Again he met the old lady. This time she chased him out of the hospital, swinging her mop at him.

Back at the paper, while going through some files, Reutlinger came across a picture of the cleaning lady. It was Mother Cabrini herself.

That was Frances Xavier Cabrini. She wasn't afraid of hard work, and she wasn't afraid of taking direct action.

She was born Maria Francesca Cabrini in a northern Italian village in 1850, the youngest of thirteen children in a prosperous farming family. As a young woman, she worked as a teacher, and later ran an orphanage. She took religious vows in 1877. Three years later, Cabrini founded a new religious order, the Missionary Sisters of the Sacred Heart of Jesus.

She had adopted the name "Xavier" to honor Saint Francis Xavier, the sixteenth-century Jesuit missionary to East Asia. Cabrini had hoped to continue his work there. However, Pope Leo XIII convinced her to go west instead. Italian immigrants had begun flooding into the United States and were having trouble adapting to their new surroundings.

Along with six other nuns, Cabrini came to New York City in 1889. She immediately ran into a problem when the house she'd planned on using for an orphanage was no longer available. The archbishop advised her to go back to Italy. Cabrini persisted and finally secured a suitable building.

Over the next decade, the work of the Missionary Sisters branched out to other cities with a large Italian population. In Chicago, Assumption Church on Illinois Street was the

Saint Frances Xavier Cabrini. *Author's collection.*

city's first Italian parish. In 1899 the pastor was planning to build a school, and asked Cabrini to run it. She agreed.

The school was an immediate success, with five hundred students enrolled for the first year. Cabrini then turned her attention to healthcare. The Italians of the city wanted a hospital that the poorest patients could afford. Cabrini found a shuttered hotel on Lakeview Avenue and purchased the building in 1903. There Cabrini demonstrated her diplomatic touch. Knowing that some Italians were frankly anticlerical and might have refused to use a religious hospital, she chose a name all Italians would appreciate— Christopher Columbus Memorial.

Columbus Hospital opened in 1903. A few years later, it was joined by a branch on the West Side. To make sure the hospital patients always had fresh food, Cabrini bought a 160-acre farm on Potter Road in what is now Park Ridge. In 1909 she became a U.S. citizen.

Finding money for the work was an ongoing task. And all the while, Cabrini was fielding requests for help from all parts of the United States, as well as from Europe and South America. She traveled widely and far, crossing the Atlantic Ocean more than twenty times. She opened schools and orphanages and convents and hospitals. In all, she was responsible for founding sixty-seven different institutions.

Always she returned to Chicago. Cabrini died in her room at Columbus Hospital on December 22, 1917. She had been preparing Christmas candy for the neighborhood children.

In the years after her death, two miracles of medical healing were attributed to Cabrini's intercession. In 1946 she was canonized by the Catholic Church. Saint Frances Xavier Cabrini was the first American citizen to have that honor.

Back in Chicago, Harry Reutlinger was still writing for the *American*. Reutlinger and Cabrini had eventually become friends. And now he had a singular distinction—he was the only reporter in the world ever chased by a mop-swinging saint.

# THE LIFE AND DEATH OF NAILS MORTON

Nails Morton wasn't your ordinary gangster. Nor was his death ordinary. And the aftermath of that death became the stuff of legend.

The oldest of seven children of Russian Jewish parents, Morton was born Samuel Marcovitz in New York in 1893. Around 1900 the family moved to the Maxwell Street area of Chicago. Marcovitz was changed to Morton at that time.

Little Sammy Morton grew into a big, brawny teenager. His neighborhood was among the poorest and most violent in Chicago, and he became involved with the local Jewish street gangs. Though he was handy with his fists, Morton's weapon of choice was a baseball bat studded with nails—which gave him a fearsome reputation, as well as a nickname.

In 1917 Morton was arrested for viciously beating several members of a Polish gang. He was found guilty of assault. At the time, World War I was raging in Europe, so the judge gave him the choice of going to prison or enlisting in the army. Morton chose the army.

"Channel those aggressive instincts!" Maybe the judge told him that. In any event, Morton found a niche in the 131st Illinois Infantry. As a government-sanctioned warrior, he led a charge against a German machine gun nest, capturing the position along with twenty prisoners while suffering two wounds. The French decorated him with the Croix de Guerre. Morton had gone into the war as a buck private. He came home a first lieutenant.

Back in Chicago, he went back to his old ways. In 1920, with Prohibition taking hold, Morton joined up with Dion O'Banion's North Side mob. O'Banion put him in charge of liquor distribution and general enforcement. The public first became acquainted with Nails Morton in 1921, when he went on trial for killing two cops and was acquitted. There was talk that jurors had been threatened or bribed.

The Maxwell Street area in 1908, around the time Nails Morton was growing up. *Author's collection.*

Morton soon became a gangland celebrity. He was seen at the city's fanciest restaurants and in the best seats at sporting events, often with a female companion or two keeping him company. He wore custom-tailored suits and drove a block-long touring car. Leaving the old neighborhood behind, he bought a graystone two-flat facing fashionable Humboldt Park.

One of Morton's mob chums, Louie Altiere, owned a three-thousand-acre ranch near Gypsum, Colorado. The ranch was a convenient place to hide fugitives from the law. But aside from that business function, the property was used for recreation. Every fall, Altiere brought his gangland associates out to the ranch for a week of hunting. During one of those visits, Morton took up horseback riding.

Morton became obsessed with the equestrian lifestyle. He bought jodhpurs, a red velvet jacket, and a black derby. When he wasn't busy shooting competitors or romancing ladies, Morton could usually be found atop a mount in Lincoln Park. By 1923 the kid from Maxwell Street was an accomplished horseman.

On the morning of May 13, he was riding through the park with some friends when one of his stirrup straps broke. The horse bolted, and Morton fell to the ground. The excited horse kicked him in the head, killing him instantly.

More than five thousand people followed the hearse that carried Morton's body along Roosevelt Road to Waldheim Cemetery. The eulogists at his brief funeral service spoke of his war heroics. They also noted that Morton had "organized a defense society to drive Jew-haters from the West Side." His other activities were passed over. On his death certificate, Morton's occupation was listed as "florist."

The North Side mob was shocked that their buddy had met death in such a prosaic manner. A few days after the funeral, Louie Altiere kidnapped the horse that had killed Morton. Altiere led the animal to the spot where Morton had fallen, then shot it dead. "We taught that damned horse of yours a lesson," he told the stable owner. "If you want the saddle, go and get it!"

For a postscript, we move forward to 1931 and the movie *The Public Enemy*. In the film, gang boss James Cagney learns that his buddy "Nails Nathan" has been killed by a horse. So, Cagney leaves Jean Harlow behind, goes to the stable, and shoots the horse.

And they say Hollywood movies aren't true to life.

## MIGHTY MILTON SILLS

Mention Milton Sills to a film historian, and many of them will draw a blank. Yet he was one of the biggest movie stars of his time. And he was a Chicagoan.

Sills was born in the city in 1882. The family had money—his father was a mineral dealer, and his mother was a banker's daughter. Milton grew up on the South Side, attended Hyde Park High School and then entered the University of Chicago in 1899. There, he studied philosophy and psychology, played sports, and joined a fraternity. He also did some acting in a few campus productions.

After graduating in 1903, he was hired by the university to teach mathematics. Sills had talked about studying for a PhD, but it's not clear what happened to that plan. What is known is that by 1905, he was a professional actor, part of a company that put on plays in Chicago and in the college towns of the Midwest.

Sills arrived on the New York stage in 1908. He spent six years there, developing his craft, before moving on to the movies. Films were still new and still silent. His screen debut in the 1914 production *The Pit* was a success, and earned him more work.

Sills was a versatile actor. He was a tall, muscular man who could play physical roles with ease. At the same time, he was an intellectual who wrote poetry, spoke four languages, and penned magazine articles without the aid of a ghostwriter. Because of this background, he also looked comfortable in the more cerebral roles.

By the 1920s he was an established leading man. Sills scored notable triumphs in *Miss Lulu Bett*, *Burning Sands*, *Adam's Rib*, and *Flaming Youth*. Film magazines called him the busiest actor in Hollywood. He was one of the highest-paid actors as well.

"The busiest actor in Hollywood," Chicago's own Milton Sills. *From the* Buffalo Enquirer, *December 2, 1922.*

Sills reached his peak with 1924's *The Sea Hawk*. The film tells the story of a fictional sixteenth-century English nobleman named Sir Oliver Tressilian. Betrayed by his own brother, Sir Oliver is shanghaied by pirates, spends time as a galley slave, and eventually emerges as the redoubtable commander of the Moorish fleet before returning home to right his wrongs and reclaim his lady love. It's a splendid swashbuckler, a worthy companion to the completely different Errol Flynn epic of the same title.

"Mighty Milton" still kept in touch with his Chicago roots. He contributed articles to the University of Chicago's alumni magazine and made regular trips home to see his widowed mother. On one such visit, hundreds of female fans mobbed him, causing a near riot.

In 1927 Sills became one of the founders of the Academy of Motion Picture Arts and Sciences. As chair of the Educational Committee, he negotiated with the University of Southern California to offer a major in film studies. Part of the committee's plan was to have directors, producers, actors, and other cinema personnel present guest lectures, which could later be shared with other colleges. Though the idea was intriguing, it was never implemented.

That same year, sound came to the movies. While many silent film stars had difficulty making the transition, for Sills, the task appeared easy— as a veteran stage actor, he knew how to deliver dialogue. Yet nothing is ever certain in the entertainment business. Sills hesitated when taking the plunge into talkies.

He took a partial plunge in 1928, when he accepted a role in *The Barker*. The film is a drama about carnival life. Like many films of the time, it's part talkie, part silent. Sills plays the title role. He has an excellent speaking voice and really can act.

Now Sills began to have health problems. He took a long vacation from work and rested in the Adirondacks. Early in 1930 he returned to Hollywood, filming *Man Trouble* and *The Sea Wolf*. On September 15, he was playing tennis with friends at his Santa Monica home when he suddenly collapsed. Efforts to revive him were futile. He was dead of a heart attack at forty-eight.

A collection of Milton Sills's thoughts on various subjects was published posthumously as *Values: A Philosophy of Human Needs*. Today he has a star on Hollywood's Walk of Fame at 6263 Hollywood Boulevard. But he is buried back in his hometown at Rosehill Cemetery.

# THE AVIATOR

Aviation was new and dangerous in the 1920s. Every time a pilot took his plane up, he was taking his life in his hands. Chicago's most celebrated aviator of those times had to overcome two additional obstacles—being a woman and being Black. Her name was Bessie Coleman.

Coleman was born in 1893, the tenth of thirteen children in a family of Texas sharecroppers. Aside from her African heritage, she was part Cherokee on her father's side. Bessie spent her childhood cotton farming and going to school when she could. At eighteen she enrolled in the Oklahoma Colored Agricultural and Normal University. She left after one semester when her money ran out.

In 1915 Coleman joined the great migration north to Chicago. She moved into an apartment with two of her brothers on Grand Boulevard (King Drive) and found work as a manicurist. Later she took a second job running a chili parlor.

Coleman was intrigued by stories of combat flying during World War I; she wanted to become a pilot herself. But when the war ended, no American flying school would accept her. Coleman had to go to France to achieve her dream.

She learned French, saved her money, and got financial help from *Chicago Defender* publisher Robert S. Abbott and other businessmen. In the fall of 1920, Coleman arrived in Paris to begin her flight training. Despite watching

# BESSIE COLEMAN

THE RACE'S ONLY

## AVIATRIX

WILL MAKE HER INITIAL
LOCAL FLIGHT AT

## CHECKERBOARD AIRDROME

## SUNDAY, OCT. 15

3 P. M. SHARP

### DIRECTIONS

METROPOLITAN "L"—Garfield Park to Forest Park station; motor bus to field.
AUTO ROUTE—West on Jackson Blvd. to Desplaines Ave., south to Roosevelt Road, west three blocks to Checkerboard Airdrome.

SEE THIS DAREDEVIL AVIATRIX
IN HER

## HAIR-RAISING STUNTS

Including French Nungesser Take-off, Spanish Berta Costa Climb, American Curtis-McMullen Turn, Eddie Rickenbacker Straighten-up, Richtofen German Glide, Ralph C. Diggins Landing. Presentation of Honor Flag to 8th Ill. Infantry. Wing Walking and Parachute Jumps

## FOUR SEPARATE FLIGHTS

AND SPECIAL PASSENGER CARRYING

Admission: Children, 25 Cents. Adults, $1.00

An advertisement for Bessie Coleman's first Chicago air show. *From the* Chicago Defender, *October 14, 1922.*

more than one fellow student die in a crash, she kept training. In June 1921 she was granted her pilot's license. She returned to the United States that September as the country's first female African American flier.

Coleman was feted as a hero by the African American press. "The air is the only place free from prejudice," she told one reporter. "You've never lived until you've flown!"

Whether Coleman's celebrity could translate into a career was another matter. With aviation in its infancy, there were no commercial pilot jobs for a Black woman. Coleman could either become a mail pilot or a stunt flier. Both were dangerous jobs, but stunt flying paid better.

So, in 1922, she went back to France for advanced flight training. When she returned home after five months, Coleman joined the circuit of air thrill shows. Coleman was young, attractive, and extroverted—performing appealed to her. In stunt flying, her gender and race worked to her advantage, giving her added publicity value.

That October she performed in Chicago for the first time. Trumpeted by the *Defender* as "The Race's Only Aviatrix," she drew a crowd of over two thousand spectators to Checkerboard Airdrome in Maywood. Coleman flew four ten-minute stints of loop-the-loops and the "Richthofen Glide." She ended the show with a hair-raising dive before bringing her craft in for a safe landing.

Coleman had discovered a new mission. "I decided Blacks should not face the difficulties I had faced," she said. "I decided to open a flying school and teach other black women to fly." Though she was determined to earn money, she would not sacrifice her dignity. She turned down a chance to star in a movie when she felt the script was demeaning to Black people.

By 1926 Coleman had established herself as a daredevil flier. On April 30 she was in Jacksonville, Florida. An air show was scheduled for the next day. With her mechanic at the controls of her open plane, Coleman took off to scout out the area. She wasn't strapped in. She wanted more freedom to see over the edge of the plane.

About ten minutes into the flight, the plane suddenly went into a spin. Coleman was thrown from the cockpit and fell to her death. The plane crashed, killing the mechanic. As it turned out, the cause of the accident was dreadfully simple—a loose wrench had fallen into the gears and jammed them.

The air show was canceled. Coleman's body was returned to Chicago, where more than ten thousand people filed past her coffin at Pilgrim Baptist Church. She was buried at Lincoln Cemetery in Alsip. For many years afterward, African American pilots performed an annual flyover of her grave.

In 1995 the U.S. Postal Service honored Chicago's aviation pioneer with a Black Heritage Commemorative Stamp. Today one of the streets at O'Hare Airport is named Bessie Coleman Drive.

# One-Eye Connelly

James Leo Connelly did not settle in the Chicago area until he was in his sixties and already celebrated in his career. Still, he had never lived in one place for very long. Besides that, his work always had a certain sort of Chicago flair. He was the world champion gate crasher.

Connelly was born in 1869 in Lowell, Massachusetts. Orphaned as a boy, he learned to live by his wits. He became a bantam-weight boxer, and all was going well until he lost an eye in a fight. From then on, he became known as One-Eye Connelly.

Although his own boxing days were over, Connelly was determined to see the Sullivan-Corbett heavyweight title bout in 1892. He talked his way into Sullivan's dressing room by claiming he had a message from the champ's brother. Sullivan liked the kid's audacity and went along with the gag.

Connelly had found his calling. From boxing, he branched out to other sports, but always the headline events—the World Series, Rose Bowl, Kentucky Derby, Stanley Cup. Connelly would be there without paying a cent for a ticket. He also favored political conventions.

His methods varied. Once, he posed as an ambulance driver arriving on a call. Another time, he was a painter doing a job outside the stadium; when Connelly asked the gatekeeper what he should paint next, the man told him to go inside to see the boss. As a variation on this ploy, he once arrived lugging a trunk that was supposedly full of newly printed tickets being delivered to the business office. Often he got into venues simply by walking quickly with an air of authority and flashing a bogus credential.

Getting places was no problem. Connelly rode the rails on every line in the country. He once stowed away on an ocean liner to reach Australia for a heavyweight title fight, then secured a return passage by getting himself deported as a Communist agitator.

He once reckoned that the most money he ever had at one time was $1,400, which he earned by hustling newspapers in the closing weeks of World War I. That bankroll enabled Connelly to seriously contemplate matrimony with someone he discreetly described as "a red-headed lady." In

A cartoon for a newspaper story about "One-Eye" Connelly. *From the* New Castle Herald, *August 19, 1922.*

the end, the marriage plans fell through. Connelly was not about to abandon his vagabond lifestyle.

He crashed gates for forty years, working only when he was hungry and, even then, only long enough to get by. He spent his winters in Florida; his summers, wherever the action was. Sportswriters loved him. They considered his antics a victimless crime that made for a light-hearted story when news was slow. Connelly returned their affection by sending Christmas cards to his favorite writers.

In 1931 he was in Waukegan when he was stricken with appendicitis. Prompt action by a county cop saved his life. Afterward, Connelly finally decided to settle down. From that point on, he was a legal resident of Zion.

He got himself a steady job, too. Connelly's wanderings had given him some culinary skills. He struck up a friendship with a politician who owned a local restaurant, and Connelly went to work there as a chef. When the restaurant went out of business, he became an elevator operator in Chicago. During World War II he worked in a defense plant.

He still crashed a few gates. Getting tired of chasing Connelly, Wrigley Field security chief Andy Frain hired him as a ticket-taker. That lasted until Connelly refused to admit a man who claimed to be Cubs owner Phil Wrigley. The man really was Phil Wrigley, and he wasn't amused having a fox guard his henhouse.

Connelly died in a Zion nursing home in 1953. At the time of his death, a *Tribune* editorial speculated he'd probably be able to sneak past St. Peter at the pearly gates. His mortal remains were interred at Ascension Cemetery in Libertyville.

*Could he still get away with crashing gates in the electronic age?* That's like asking if Babe Ruth, Jack Dempsey, or Jesse Owens could still be stars in their sports. Talent finds a way, no matter what the era. One-Eye Connelly would find a way. You can put your money on that.

## ARCHITECT OF THE GOOD LIFE

In Chicago, architects have always been celebrities. Sullivan, Burnham, Wright, Mies van der Rohe—the names readily come to mind. There is also Benjamin Howard Marshall. Though not as well-remembered as the others, Marshall left a lasting imprint on the city.

Marshall was born into a wealthy South Side family in 1874. As a boy he loved animals and would often smuggle pets into school. Once, he even brought a pony to church. Ben Marshall would always do things his own way. He was talented enough, charming enough, and rich enough to carry it off.

While he was in high school, Marshall was impressed by the grand buildings of the Columbian Exposition. He decided to become an architect. Rather than waste time in musty academic studies, he apprenticed himself to a local design office. A few years later he opened his own firm.

He set out to build large public buildings, but his first major commission nearly became his last. Marshall's Iroquois Theater opened in the Loop on November 23, 1903. Little more than a month later, the Iroquois was destroyed by a fire, and over six hundred lives were lost. The official investigation cleared the architect of responsibility for the tragedy.

Marshall's career soon rebounded. In 1905 he went into partnership with Charles E. Fox. The two men complemented each other. With formal training in architecture at MIT, Fox was what one writer called the "nuts-and-bolts guy." Marshall was the visionary designer, whose personal charisma helped cultivate wealthy clients.

Over the next two decades, the firm of Marshall and Fox produced such Chicago landmarks as the Blackstone Hotel, Lake Shore National Bank, the Edgewater Beach Hotel, South Shore Country Club, and the Drake Hotel. The partners also built many stylish Gold Coast apartments, including five of the eight buildings on East Lake Shore Drive. Marshall himself designed a few private residences for those who could afford his work. The most famous of these was the Samuel Insull estate in Vernon Hills, now the Cuneo Museum.

Marshall cut a flamboyant figure. He designed much of his personal wardrobe, which included elaborately ruffled shirts, flowing ties, and—for the golf course—a large sombrero with built-in ventilators. He drove a white, customized Packard convertible. On one occasion, Marshall threw a party for the entire cast of the Ziegfeld Follies. He had money and he spent it, all the while giving the impression that if he didn't have it, he would have spent it anyway.

O Rare Ben Marshall.
*Author's collection.*

The 1550 North State Apartments is a fine example of Marshall's style. Its opulent Second Empire design suggests it might have easily been placed on the Champs Elysees, and in fact, Marshall labeled his plans in French. When the building opened in 1911, it was considered the height of luxury.

Each of the twelve floors had only a single apartment, a living space of nine thousand square feet divided into fifteen rooms. The rooms facing east and north had magnificent views of the lake and Lincoln Park. The windows were fronted with iron balconies. Even the appliances were special—the kitchen ranges had three broilers, two gas and one charcoal, "so that steaks and fish need never be prepared on the same broiler."

Marshall lived in the 1550 building for nine years. Then he built a combination home and office complex in Wilmette. Included in the thirty-two-room main building was an entire room from a Chinese temple and an architectural studio large enough to accommodate a staff of forty-five. The grounds featured a tropical garden and an Egyptian solarium. The property was so lavish, it was listed as an attraction in Chicago guidebooks.

The partnership with Fox was dissolved in 1924, and Marshall continued on as a solo architect. His most notable commission from this period was the Edgewater Beach Apartments. Constructed just north of the hotel in 1928, the sunset-pink building escaped the demolition that claimed its neighbor, and still stands on Sheridan Road.

The Great Depression hit Marshall hard. He filed for bankruptcy in 1934, sold off his Wilmette holdings, and moved into a suite at the Drake Hotel. He died there in 1944. Today the Benjamin Marshall Society works to highlight his achievements.

# THE CONSTANT CANDIDATE

I first learned the meaning of the word *incumbent* when I was eleven years old. It was the evening of the 1959 Chicago mayoral primary. Grandpa Price was a Democratic Party precinct captain, and while he was off doing whatever he was doing, the rest of the family listened to the returns over the radio. Every fifteen minutes or so, I would hear the announcer say something like, "Daley, the incumbent, 244,978 votes. Lar Daly, 302 votes."

So, *incumbent* referred to the current mayor, Richard J. Daley. But who or what was a Lar Daly?

Lawrence Joseph Sarsfield Daly, that's who. He was born in 1912, lived on the South Side, was married and had five children. He operated a business that sold barstools. What made Lar Daly famous locally was his hobby. He ran for public office—and lost. He did it about thirty times.

Strangely enough, in his first campaign, Daly actually won. In 1932 he was elected a Republican ward committeeman. Then it was discovered that he was only twenty years old and not eligible for the job.

He next ran for Cook County superintendent of schools in the 1938 Democratic primary. He began using the name "Lar" because he thought it would win him some Swedish votes. It didn't work, and his losing streak began.

Daly was an equal-opportunity candidate. He ran on whichever ticket gave him the best shot at victory. In that 1959 mayoral primary, he was a candidate in both the Democratic and Republican contests.

In philosophy he was a Libertarian. He favored legalized gambling, was against public education, and called for major tax cuts. He was also a staunch isolationist—he billed himself as Lar "America First" Daly. Often he campaigned while wearing an Uncle Sam suit.

People who knew him well liked him. He played the fiddle and loved to entertain friends at parties. He was also a pretty good public speaker with a rich baritone voice.

Still, it was hard to take him seriously. At one outdoor gathering, Daly was dressed in his Uncle Sam costume, telling the audience what was wrong with government. He was running through the list, saying, "Point one… point two."

Then a heckler yelled, "Why don't you take off that hat and show us point three?"

In a way, Daly was responsible for the development of modern presidential debates. Federal law then said that radio and TV stations had to grant equal

A campaign button for Lar "America First" Daly. *Author's collection.*

time to all the candidates for an office. Daly routinely filed appeals when he was denied access—and in 1959, the Federal Communications Commission ruled in his favor! Local Chicago stations were forced to give him free airtime, and Congress was forced to rewrite the laws in question. When Kennedy and Nixon squared off in their historic 1960 debates, Lar Daly was nowhere to be seen.

So, he went on, running and losing—in 1962 for the U.S. Senate; in 1963 for mayor of Chicago; in 1964 for governor of Illinois; in 1966 again for the U.S. Senate; in 1967 for mayor of Chicago; in 1969 for the Thirteenth Congressional District special election; and so on, and so on.

In 1973 Daly won the Republican primary for the Seventh Congressional District special election. That wasn't hard to do, as he was running unopposed in a heavily Democratic district. In the general election, he was clobbered.

Politics costs money, even at Daly's level. During the 1970s, he began appearing without the Uncle Sam suit. Rumor was that he'd had to pawn it.

His last campaign was the Republican U.S. Senate primary in 1978. Running against Charles Percy, Daly polled 74,779 votes; at 15 percent, it was his best showing in years in a contested election. A month later, Lar Daly was dead.

Today he remains a legend among local political junkies. A story I heard a few years ago confirms this. In 1948, Governor Harold Stassen of Minnesota almost became the Republican nominee for president of the United States. That near miss did something to Stassen. For decades afterward, he ran a string of unsuccessful campaigns and eventually became a national joke. So, when Stassen died, a Chicago commentator was asked to describe him.

His response was classic—Harold Stassen had been "a big-time Lar Daly."

# MISS FRANCES

Before there was Mister Rogers, there was Miss Frances.

She started life as Frances Rappaport, the daughter of an Austrian immigrant who owned a local general store in small-town Ohio, in 1907. She became known as Frances Horwich after her 1931 marriage to Harvey Horwich, an attorney. During the next dozen years, Frances held various jobs in education while pursuing graduate study. She earned her doctorate at Northwestern University in 1942.

In 1946 Dr. Frances Horwich became the chair of the Department of Education at the new Roosevelt College in Chicago. She was still there in 1952, when local station WMAQ-TV decided to produce a half-hour children's show as an experiment. Frances was hired as the show's host.

*Ding-Dong School* premiered on October 2, 1952. Though some executives had been skeptical about the idea, public response to the show was enthusiastic, and the station put it on its regular weekday morning schedule. By the end of November, WMAQ-TV's parent network, NBC, had picked up the program for national broadcast.

The show's target audience was preschool and kindergarten-age children. The show began with Miss Frances ringing a school bell while singing her theme song. Then she'd greet her viewers. She spoke slowly, clearly, and warmly. She talked to the children at their level. But she didn't talk down to them.

The show's content was varied. Miss Frances might demonstrate how to make something out of clay, or blow bubbles, or talk about pictures. She'd show viewers how everyday items like handkerchiefs or socks could be used for imaginative play. The show contained practical lessons, too. In one surviving kinescope, she takes children through the steps of constructing a peanut butter and lettuce sandwich.

Miss Frances aimed to educate adults as well as children. As the show wound down to its last five minutes, the children would be told to bring their mothers, fathers, or other guardians to the TV set. Then Miss Frances would explain some of the things she'd done on the program that day and why she did them. For instance, though adults must do all the cutting in the sandwich recipe, the children were told they should do the spreading and patting down. That gave the kids a feeling of participation.

Just as it had been locally, *Ding Dong School* was an immediate national sensation. Within weeks it was drawing an audience in excess of 2 million viewers. The *New York Post* said it was "the first network TV program really conceived to meet the preschool child's needs." The show won a Peabody Award for distinguished achievement in media and earned four separate Emmy nominations.

The program also made Frances Horwich a celebrity. Children would see her on the street and start singing the show's theme song. More than a few of them were puzzled that she appeared not in black-and-white, but in color. She took it all in good humor, chatting with her fans and signing autographs on anything that was thrust in front of her. Her husband took everything in good humor, too—he began calling himself "Mister Frances."

*Ding Dong School* continued to be broadcast from Chicago after NBC picked it up for national airing. But in 1955, Miss Frances was hired by the network as its director of children's programing. That meant she had to move to New York.

The program's success had led to a number of product spin-offs. Aside from the dozens of *Ding Dong School* storybooks, there were *Ding Dong School* pencils, chalk sticks, 45-rpm records, trunks, tom-toms, school bells, and even patterns for making a children's aprons. Miss Frances saw nothing wrong with this form of merchandizing as long as the goods were educational and safe.

That restriction eventually led to conflict with the network. According to the usual narrative, a BB-gun manufacturer wanted to become a sponsor, but Miss Frances vetoed him. There were also reports that she refused a request to expand the show to one hour. In any event, NBC dropped *Ding Dong School* in the spring of 1956.

Miss Frances then returned to Chicago. Over the next few decades, she was involved in a number of educational activities, including a syndicated reboot of *Ding Dong School*. She retired to Arizona in the 1990s. She died there in 2001.

Dr. Frances Horwich had no children. But Miss Frances had millions of them.

# MILE-A-MINUTE HARRY

The TV series *Mr. Selfridge* told the story of the American expat who founded an iconic London department store. The show occasionally mentioned Selfridge's years "back in Chicago." Here is that backstory.

Born in 1858, Harry Gordon Selfridge grew up in Jackson, Michigan. His father abandoned the family, and Harry left school at fourteen. He worked in a bank, in a furniture factory, in an insurance agency. Whatever the job, he impressed his bosses with his energy, intelligence, and imagination.

At twenty-one, he came to Chicago with a letter of introduction to merchant prince Marshall Field. Field put him to work as a stock boy at ten dollars a week. By 1883 Harry had moved up to a junior executive position in the retail department.

Almost immediately, Selfridge clashed with the store's traditionalists. Rather than merely supplying a product, his idea was to make shopping a recreational experience—what we today call "retail therapy." That meant aggressive marketing and all-out promotion. Field himself was naturally conservative, but Selfridge convinced the big boss to give his methods a try.

Selfridge increased advertising fivefold and launched a series of "special sales." Merchandise was hauled out from behind counters and placed on tables for easy browsing. Window displays became elaborate. A bargain basement was opened. Then came a ladies' tearoom.

There was always something new. Selfridge could usually be found on the sales floor, checking every little thing or lending his ear to the shoppers. He worked his staff hard, but he worked himself harder. When he had to criticize a subordinate, he did so privately, and that was appreciated. And since most of the innovations worked, Field was pleased. In 1887 he made Selfridge retail general manager. Two years later, "Mile-a-Minute Harry" became a junior partner.

Selfridge wore his prosperity well. Always immaculately dressed, he changed clothes two or three times a day. Most mornings a barber came to his office to groom him. In 1890 he married Rosalie Buckingham, a society debutante from the Buckingham Fountain family. The ceremony was held at the Central Music Hall, with a fifty-voice chorus providing the music. The couple later built a vacation villa on Lake Geneva.

Marshall Field & Co.'s sales continue to grow. But as he moved into middle age, Harry Selfridge was restless. He'd always wanted to run his own store. Early in 1904, he saw his opportunity. The owners of the Schlesinger & Mayer store, a block down State Street, were looking to sell.

## The Birth of a New Business.

This morning at 8 o'clock we assume ownership and control of the business which for many years under the name of Schlesinger & Mayer has been located at this corner of State and Madison-sts. . . . . Hereafter this beautiful building will be occupied by H. G. Selfridge & Co., which firm name we shall endeavor to make favorably known to every man, woman and child in Chicago and in this part of America.

\* \* \* \* \* \*

The policy of the house will be: ABSOLUTE INTEGRITY—SATISFAC-TION—ACCOMMODATION—with the purpose of winning and holding the CONFIDENCE of every individual who enters its doors.

\* \* \* \* \* \*

Under no possible circumstances will this house sanction any word or deed of any employe designed to mislead a purchaser.

\* \* \* \* \* \*

Whenever mistakes happen—as happen they must—the house will consider it a privilege to correct them with promptitude and courtesy.

\* \* \* \* \* \*

The spirit of ACCOMMODATION will rule, and in the treatment of patrons and visitors this spirit will be developed to the fullest possible extent.

\* \* \* \* \* \*

These are a few of the principles—the foundation stones—upon which this new business will stand. But greatest of all is that unequaled principle—that unshakable rock—TRUE INTEGRITY, upon which everlasting foundation this business will be fixed so firmly that it will become as a part of the rock itself.

\* \* \* \* \* \*

Furthermore, we shall see to it that our stocks are put into the best possible condition as soon as it can be done, and to this end our early duty will be to clear the shelves and reserve rooms of certain parts of the stocks now on hand. We shall therefore, as quickly as possible, make a number of sharp reductions in prices of such goods as must be sold—a work which will begin this morning and continue until the desired result is accomplished.

We may add that no formal opening is possible at present. This important event will occur next fall, due notice of which will be published.

*We therefore extend to all in and around Chicago a most cordial invitation to count this store as their own—to be free to feel perfectly at home here—to depend upon it—to criticise it to its managers, by which criticisms we expect continually to improve it and to make it more and more as you, the public, would like it.*

*H. G. Selfridge & Co.*

Harry Selfridge announces the grand opening of his new State Street store. *From the* Chicago Inter-Ocean, *June 13, 1904.*

That May, Harry broke the news to his boss. "Mr. Field, I have decided to go into business for myself," he said. "I am going to buy Schlesinger and Mayer's interest." Though Field might have anticipated this day, he was not happy about it. He wished Harry luck in a perfunctory manner, then went about his business. Afterward he grumbled, "Now we'll have to get another office boy."

The price for Schlesinger & Mayer was $5 million. Selfridge cashed in his $1.5 million worth of Marshall Field's stock and quickly rounded up the rest to seal the deal. In June, H.G. Selfridge & Co. staged a lavish grand opening. As a brass band played, the new proprietor stood on the store roof and personally ran up the house flag.

Within weeks, Selfridge realized he'd bitten off more than he could chew. He was severely undercapitalized. Like many a boss before or since, he discovered that his employees were not willing to work as hard as he was. And after twenty-five years, he found it uncomfortable going head to head against Marshall Field's in wooing customers. "I feel as if I am competing with my own people," he said.

Fortunately, Samuel Pirie of Carson Pirie Scott was looking for a presence on State Street. In August, H.G. Selfridge & Co. sold out to the Carson interests for the same $5 million that had been paid to Schlesinger & Mayer. On top of this, Harry received a personal bonus of $150,000. That last bit of coin led him to boast, "I am the only man ever to buy a business from five Jews and sell it to seven Scotchmen at a profit."

Harry spent the next few years playing golf. In 1909 he opened his London store. From that point on, we can turn it back to the TV show.

## Joseph Medill's Last Words

There's always been a fascination about the last words of famous people. We are told that when Julius Caesar was set upon by assassins and noticed his friend Brutus among them, he said, "Et tu, Brute?" ("And you also, Brutus?") Generations of American schoolchildren learned that Nathan Hale's last words before being hanged by the British were: "I regret that I have but one life to give for my country." Likewise, French kids were taught that Napoleon's dying declaration was: "France…the army…the head of the army…Josephine."

A celebrity's last words—actually, a single last word—drive the plot of a classic film. *Citizen Kane* (1941) is about a fictional American newspaper tycoon, Charles Foster Kane. The opening scene shows Kane on his deathbed, muttering "rosebud" before passing away. The rest of the movie tells the story of Kane's life in flashback as a reporter unsuccessfully tries to uncover the meaning of that enigmatic word. (Spoiler Alert: "Rosebud" was the sled eight-year-old Charlie Kane was playing with when he suddenly had great wealth thrust on him.)

The character Charles Foster Kane was famously modeled after William Randolph Hearst. But for the most notable last words of a real-life newspaper mogul, we turn to Joseph Medill.

Medill was born in Canada in 1823 and grew up in Ohio. After starting off in the newspaper business in Cleveland, he moved to Chicago in 1855, buying a stake in the *Tribune*. He later gained majority control of the paper and took over as editor-in-chief.

In Chicago, Medill became active in politics. He was an influential Republican Party power broker and a close friend of Abraham Lincoln. (Medill's second-most famous quotation was spoken to Lincoln: "Abe, get your damn feet off my desk!") In 1871, in the aftermath of the Great Fire,

Joseph Medill in his old age. *Author's collection.*

Medill was elected mayor of Chicago on the "Fire-Proof" ticket. But he resigned the office before the end of his two-year term and went back to running the *Tribune*.

As he entered his seventies, Medill's health began to decline. In 1894 he suffered a heart attack. He had regular kidney and prostate problems. He retreated from the harsh Midwestern winters, establishing a California ranch near Pasadena. He was also spending less time at his Chicago townhouse and more time at his country estate near Wheaton.

There is a famous photograph from these years of Medill with his four grown grandchildren. Each of them went on to have noteworthy careers. Joseph Medill Patterson was a founder and first editor of the *New York Daily News*. Eleanor "Cissy" Patterson became the first woman to head a major American daily newspaper, the *Washington Times-Herald*. Medill McCormick was elected a United States senator from Illinois. And rounding out the group was Robert R. McCormick, old Joe's favorite, who was known as Bertie.

In the fall of 1898, Joseph Medill left Chicago for his customary winter sojourn. Bertie had taken a semester off from school to accompany him. After arriving in San Antonio, they checked into a suite at the Manger Hotel, next to the Alamo. This time, the warm climate didn't seem to help Medill. He seldom left his room. He developed a kidney infection and required medical care.

Medill was dying, and he knew he was dying. On the morning of March 16, 1899, a physician attended him in the suite. Shortly after 10:00 a.m., Medill called the doctor over to his bedside. Then he said, "My last words shall be—'What is the news?'" After that, Medill spoke no more. Within ten minutes, he was dead.

Now that's what you call dedication to your craft. Here is Medill approaching death, and he is thinking about what will be catchy in the next day's newspapers. Notice that he announces: "My last words shall be." Medill wanted to make sure the doctor knew what was coming after that, would remember the words, and would pass them on.

Robert R. "Bertie" McCormick eventually followed in his grandfather's footsteps as the longtime editor-publisher of the *Chicago Tribune*. And today, you can find Joseph Medill's last words listed in nearly every collection of famous farewells—just as he wanted them to be.

## 3.

# POLITICS AND POLITICOS

## Who Was Dan Ryan?

Chicago has four major expressways. Three are named in honor of famous people. To the northwest, the Kennedy Expressway is named for the charismatic president of the United States who was gunned down in the prime of his life. To the west, the Eisenhower Expressway is named for a beloved president who'd also been a renowned general in World War II. To the southwest, the Stevenson Expressway is named for an Illinois governor who might have become president but lost twice to that renowned general.

To the south, the Ryan Expressway is named for a Chicago politician. His name was Dan Ryan, and this is who he was.

Born in Chicago in 1894, Daniel Ryan Jr. grew up on the city's South Side. He came from a political family; Daniel Ryan Sr. was active in the local Democratic Party, eventually becoming president of the Cook County Board of Commissioners. Meanwhile, young Dan served in the navy during World War I and earned a law degree from Chicago-Kent College of Law.

Dan Ryan Sr. died in 1923. The county board honored him by naming the forest preserve at Eighty-Seventh Street and Western Avenue the Dan Ryan Woods. Dan Ryan Jr. was appointed to his father's seat on the board, finished the term, then left to run the family insurance business. In 1930 he ran for the board in his own right and was elected. He was there for the rest of his life.

Dan Ryan was a Democratic machine politician, with all the baggage that implies. He formed alliances with various factions and gradually built a power base. As early as 1933, when Anton Cermak was killed, Ryan was in the running to be slated as the mayor of Chicago but was passed over. His fondest ambition was to become governor of Illinois. He never made that office either.

"He lacked the ruthless ambition to reach the top," one writer said. "He sat in on all the inner circle meetings but usually more as a spectator than a manipulator." Still, he got things done. Ryan was a big, bluff, hearty man who had few enemies. Republicans were still a factor in local politics, and he got along famously with them.

In 1954 Dan matched his father by being elected Cook County Board president. County government was politically charged then—just as it had been in the past, just as it is today. But Ryan managed his fellow board members with a firm hand. During his tenure, there were no major scandals.

Sometimes he rose above politics. When the University of Illinois trustees wanted to take over a big chunk of the forest preserve for a new campus, Ryan stopped them cold. At another board meeting, a scientist requested money to buy cages for research dogs. Ryan was a dog lover. His response was: "The only use we could make of such cages is to put research scientists in them."

Ryan suffered from asthma all his life. In the spring of 1961, he showed up at a political meeting wheezing and breathing heavily. Everyone noticed. "You fellows are looking at me like I'm going to die," he snapped. "Well, I'll tell you something—I'll be around to be a candidate at the next election."

That was on Thursday. On Friday the asthma was worse, and Ryan went home to rest. On Saturday morning he had a heart attack. He was taken to the hospital and died a few hours later. The date was April 8, 1961. He was sixty-six years old.

Ryan's death was front-page news in all four of Chicago's papers. The other politicians issued the usual flowery statements of regret, but most of them seemed genuinely grieved by his passing. At the funeral, the most notable mourner was TV star Danny Thomas. Ryan had been a staunch supporter of Saint Jude Children's Hospital, Thomas's favorite charity, and the two men had become personal friends.

A while later, someone recalled that Ryan had proposed using county funds to build a "superhighway" back in 1939. Now that he was gone, what better memorial than to name the new South Expressway after him? So, it was done.

And that's who Dan Ryan was.

# BLOND BOSS BILLY

In 2012, former Illinois governor Rod Blagojevich began serving a fourteen-year sentence in federal prison. He had been convicted of trying to sell the U.S. Senate seat that was being vacated by president-elect Barack Obama.

Yet buying your way into the Senate was nothing new. The most notorious case of this took place exactly one hundred years before the Blagojevich matter. And as you might expect, a Chicago politician was in the middle of it. His name was William Lorimer.

Lorimer was an Englishman, born in Manchester in 1861. He grew up in poverty on the West Side of Chicago. After running through a series of jobs, he started to make some serious money manufacturing bricks and trading real estate.

People liked Billy Lorimer. He was charming, and he was smart. He eventually went into Republican politics and was elected to the U.S. House of Representatives in 1894.

Even while he was in Washington, Congressman Lorimer never forgot his home base. He built a powerful political bloc on the West Side, which he ran like a general. The press called him the Blond Boss. He was involved in some fishy deals but always managed to wiggle out of trouble.

In 1909 United States senators were still chosen by the legislature of each state. One of the two senators from Illinois was scheduled to start a new six-year term that March. So, in January, the Illinois legislature began voting on whom they'd send to Washington. The vote deadlocked. Weeks passed—sixty, seventy, eighty ballots. March came, the Senate convened in Washington, and Illinois was still short a senator.

At first Lorimer wasn't even considered. Then one of his allies introduced his name as a compromise candidate. On the ninety-fifth ballot, Blond Billy was elected. Nearly half of his votes came from the Democratic side of the aisle.

Lorimer was seated by the Senate in June. A year later, the *Tribune* dropped a political bombshell—one of the legislators confessed that he had been paid $1,000 to vote for Lorimer. The man claimed that other legislators had also been bribed.

Lorimer demanded that the Senate investigate the charges. A committee was formed, came to Illinois, held hearings, and cleared him. The committee did find bribery in connection to Lorimer's election but said Lorimer hadn't known about it. Anyway, those bribed votes hadn't mattered; Lorimer's

Senator Billy Lorimer, the Blond Boss. *Author's collection.*

winning margin was so large, he would have been elected without them. Therefore, there was no reason to throw him out of the Senate. In March 1911, the full Senate voted. Lorimer kept his seat, with a vote of 46–40.

Meanwhile, back in Illinois, new information was surfacing. Lorimer's buddies had laid out over $100,000 in bribes to ensure his election. One Chicago businessman had put $10,000 into the pot because he knew Lorimer favored a high tariff. Now the Illinois legislature was launching its own probe of the 1909 Senate vote. In June 1911, the U.S. Senate appointed a second committee to investigate Lorimer's election. After six months, the second committee also cleared him.

But by then, Lorimer was becoming an embarrassment. The Republicans were running for cover. Ex-president Roosevelt refused to attend a party fundraiser until the senator was uninvited. Vice president Sherman publicly asked Lorimer to resign.

Defiantly, Lorimer said he would fight on. He was being smeared because of politics. The newspapers were out to get him. He was the champion of the people. He had been honestly elected to do the people's business. He wasn't a quitter—he wouldn't quit!

On July 13, 1912, the full Senate once again voted on the Lorimer case. The senator claimed that he was being subjected to double jeopardy, that he had already been cleared once by the Senate. His arguments were ignored. The report of the second committee was also ignored. Senator Billy Lorimer was expelled by a vote of 55–28.

The stink of the Lorimer case led to a change in the U.S. Constitution. The Seventeenth Amendment was quickly adopted and went into effect in 1913. Now U.S. Senators were to be directly elected by the people. Surely that would end the bribery and fraud.

Billy Lorimer never held another political office. In 1934 he was found dead in the washroom at the Chicago & North Western Railway terminal.

# The Rosemont Corridor

The city of Chicago sprawls over 234 square miles. Most of that land was acquired by simple growth and annexation. Occasionally the process has been acrimonious. One notorious incident took place in 1899, when Chicago and Cicero Township teamed up in a referendum to make the town of Austin part of the city against the will of Austin's voters.

A more recent tale of the city's expansion involves a tiny sliver of land we will call the Rosemont Corridor. In its own way, it is a classic example of Chicago politics at work.

In 1942 World War II was underway, and the Douglas Aircraft Corporation built a plant on government land, near the farm village of Orchard Place, at Mannheim and Higgins Roads. When the war ended in 1945, the feds transferred 1,080 acres to the City of Chicago. The property became the city's second airport, Orchard Field—or ORD. A few years later, the name of the facility was changed to O'Hare Airport.

Though Chicago held title to the airport's property, the site itself was a few miles beyond the city limits on unincorporated land. That fact might cause legal complications. Since the airport was technically outside of Chicago, there was a question about whether city ordinances could be enforced there. *Could the city charge license fees to businesses operating at the airport? Could the Chicago Police even issue parking tickets?* Of course, if that airport land were directly connected to the rest of the city, there wouldn't be a problem.

Early in 1956, the Chicago City Council opened hearings on formally annexing the land between the city limits and the airport. Part of the plan was for Chicago to annex forest preserve acreage along the Des Plaines River. At the same time, the city would annex a three-mile-long, sixty-six-foot-wide strip of Higgins Road. This narrow corridor would stretch from the existing Chicago border at Canfield Avenue to the airport land at Mannheim Road. The shoestring link might look strange on paper, but there was precedent for it in other cities. Chicago would then have its physical connection to O'Hare.

The Cook County Board was controlled by Chicago Democrats, so annexation of the forest preserve land was easily done. Most of the property along Higgins Road and the surrounding area was vacant, and Chicago officials had reckoned that the annexation would go smoothly there as well. Yet, out on the prairie, the homesteaders in Park Ridge and Des Plaines were alarmed. Those Chicago city slickers were invading their territory. *What would happen to their peaceful country lives?*

Now both Park Ridge and Des Plaines began planning their own annexations, trying to block Chicago's land grab. The newly incorporated village of Rosemont followed suit. To help things along, Leyden Township officials volunteered to coordinate the new suburban borders.

Mayor Richard J. Daley of Chicago wasn't about to let a few little hamlets interfere with the greater good of a city of 3.6 million people. On March 28, Daley met with officials from the rebellious suburbs behind closed doors. When the meeting ended, he announced that the matter was settled. Chicago's annexation of Higgins Road would go forward.

By virtue of that strip along Higgins—which was only thirty-three feet wide in some places—O'Hare Airport became an integral part of the city of Chicago. But the solution proved to be temporary. In 1959, in a different case, the Illinois Supreme Court raised questions about the legality of those shoestring annexations.

Daley did not wait for the court to take up the Higgins annexation. He struck a deal with Rosemont to swap his Higgins Road strip in exchange for a 185-foot-deep strip along Foster Avenue, on Rosemont's southern border with Schiller Park. If there were other considerations involved, they weren't reported. The matter finally was settled.

The Rosemont Corridor, Foster Avenue, looking west from River Road. *Photograph by the author.*

Today there's nothing to identify the little corridor along Foster as part of Chicago, except for a few city streetlights. The old suburban street signs are still in place. And in a final bit of irony, the Rosemont land to the north has undergone massive redevelopment, while the Chicago land is occupied by single-story industrial buildings.

# THE FIRST CULLERTON

Chicago is known for its dynastic politics, most famously in the case of the Mayors Daley, father and son. In an earlier era, there were the Mayors Harrison, father and son. But in terms of length of public service—or numbers of public servants—no Chicago family can compete with the Cullerton clan.

P.J. "Parky" Cullerton was a Chicago alderman and Cook County assessor. William Cullerton was also an alderman—so were Thomas Cullerton and Timothy Cullerton. John Cullerton served in both houses of the state legislature, including eleven years as president of the Illinois Senate. There has also been at least one Cullerton daughter and one son-in-law in the political mix.

It all goes back to the dynasty's founding father, Edward Francis Cullerton.

He was born on a farm near what is now suburban Summit on October 11, 1842, the son of Irish immigrant parents who'd come to America the year before. At twelve young Eddy quit school to go to work in a brickyard. Later he kept a livery stable, then spent ten years as a pilot on the Illinois and Michigan Canal, eventually buying his own boat. For a few years he lived in Canada.

He returned to Chicago for good in 1871. That October, the Great Fire leveled much of the city. A month after the fire, *Tribune* publisher Joseph Medill was elected mayor on the "Fire-Proof" ticket. Also elected was a new Democratic alderman from the Lower West Side, the Honorable E.F. Cullerton.

He took to politics quickly. A year after his election to the council, Cullerton was elected to the Illinois House of Representatives. He continued to serve as alderman while serving as state representative—since both offices were part time and low paying, that kind of double-dipping was perfectly legal then. But soon Cullerton discovered that his time in Springfield had forced him to neglect his Chicago business interests, and he left the General

Assembly after a single term. He later turned down slating for the Illinois Senate and for the U.S. House of Representatives.

Cullerton preferred the personal connection of local politics. In his early campaigns, he typically traveled through the ward, along with his wife, in a horse-drawn buggy. He'd stop at an intersection, attract a crowd, and make a speech. Every two years, his neighbors responded with their votes.

As the years went by, however, the alderman became a target of the good government reformers. In 1892, sensing a tough reelection fight, he managed to get the endorsement of both the Democratic and Republican Parties. But when the votes were counted, Cullerton had lost.

Six years later, the voters gave him his old job back. More years passed, and Cullerton became chairman of the Finance Committee, the council's most powerful post. Solidifying his reputation for political astuteness, he was always careful with his words, never speaking a sentence when a single word would do and never speaking a single word unless it was necessary. The newspapers called him Silent Ed, Smooth Ed and, most often, Foxy Ed.

As mentioned, being an alderman was only a part-time job. Throughout his career, Cullerton was involved in many ventures. From 1878 to 1882, he operated a wholesale liquor business in partnership with another alderman. Then he owned a roofing company. In 1901 the city directory listed Cullerton's

Edward F. Cullerton's home on Twentieth Street—now Cullerton Street. *Photograph by the author.*

occupation as "detective." In 1903 he was called a "real estate broker." The 1905 directory said Cullerton was head of the Chicago Tax Adjusting Company. He also published a weekly newspaper called *The Taxpayer*.

Early in 1914 the alderman became seriously ill and nearly died. Still, his health improved enough for him to again win reelection that April. In his later years, he ran solely on his past record, with no platform. "I make no re-election promises," he said in a rare speech. "I judge each ordinance or resolution when it comes up and in the light of the circumstances that then exist."

On February 1, 1920, Alderman Edward F. Cullerton passed away at his home on Twentieth Street. The cause of death was pneumonia. A few weeks later, the city council changed the name of Twentieth Street to Cullerton Street.

# WHY THE KENNEDY CURVES AT DIVISION STREET

When driving northwest from downtown on the Kennedy Expressway, you come to a curve in the roadway just past Augusta Boulevard. Now the expressway runs straight north for a few blocks, skirting close to some adjacent buildings and crossing over Division Street on a viaduct. Then another curve brings the Kennedy back to its earlier course. Why the expressway curves here is a bit of Chicago history that even many historians get wrong.

As early as 1927, planners were talking about building an express highway to the northwest from downtown Chicago. The Avondale Avenue Superhighway would run adjacent to the Chicago & North Western Railway's (C&NW) northwest branch line. The Great Depression, and then World War II, stalled the plan.

In 1946, with the war over, the project got moving. There were no federal interstate highway funds then, so the city, county, and state were paying for the $177 million project now known as the Northwest Expressway. As in the earlier plans, the new road's right of way would be along the west side of the C&NW tracks.

North of Division Street, the expressway was routed through a heavily populated Polish area. The road was to be depressed below street level, passing in front of Saint Stanislaus Kostka Church at 1327 North Noble Street. Dozens of buildings would be demolished, and the historic church would be cut off from much of the neighborhood.

The Kennedy Expressway curve at Division Street, with Saint Stan's visible in the background. *Photograph by the author.*

The Poles were Chicago's largest ethnic group. No politician wanted to alienate that many voters. What looked good on the drawing board wasn't always practical. So, on December 13, Governor Dwight Green announced a revised route for the expressway. At Augusta Boulevard, the road would swing east over the C&NW tracks on a bridge, then continue north on a viaduct directly over Elston Avenue for a distance of a little over a mile. Near Armitage Avenue, another bridge would carry the expressway back over to the west side of the railroad.

No price tag for the revised route was mentioned. "The state is glad to agree to this change because the original route cut through the center of the Polish district and would have adversely affected churches and other established institutions," the governor said. "We feel that the protection of community interests justifies the increased expense." That appeared to end the controversy.

Years passed. By 1955, work on the Northwest Expressway was finally ready to begin. The state then decided that the Elston Viaduct was too expensive. The highway would follow the cheapest route along the west side of the C&NW line. Under this plan, Saint Stanislaus itself would have to be bulldozed.

Meanwhile, onetime State Representative Bernard Prusinski was feuding with Thirty-Second Ward alderman Joseph Rostenkowski. That spring

Prusinski had run for alderman on a "Save Saint Stan's" platform. Though Rostenkowski was a longtime incumbent, Prusinski's message resonated, and he won the election. Once in office, the new alderman went to work getting the expressway moved—again.

Prusinski was a civil engineer by profession. He came up with a plan to curve the C&NW tracks a few hundred yards east, onto land that was mostly vacant. The new expressway would then be built along the west line of the relocated railroad tracks. The additional cost would be minor, and the mother church of Chicago Poles would be preserved.

The state agreed to fund the change. So today, when you travel the Kennedy Expressway, you can see where the road curves around the church, just as Prusinski had proposed. Yet there's a final bit of irony here.

In 1958 Joseph Rostenkowski's son Dan was elected to the U.S. House of Representatives. Dan Rostenkowski stayed in Congress for thirty-six years and became a power on Capitol Hill. All that time he maintained a residence in the old neighborhood, a block from Saint Stanislaus.

Somewhere along the line, the legend developed that the congressman had been the person who'd saved Saint Stanislaus from the wrecker's ball. And now that stretch of expressway near the church, which helped drive Dan Rostenkowski's father from office, is nicknamed Rosty's Curve.

## STARRING MARTIN KENNELLY

Martin Kennelly looked like a statesman. Tall, handsome, white-haired, and somber, he gave off a vibe of quiet dignity. He might have been the movie version of a senator or an ambassador—or perhaps even president of the United States.

Martin Kennelly was actually the mayor of Chicago. During most of his two terms in office, he did seem more like an actor who was simply playing the role.

Like Ed Kelly before him and Daley Senior after him, Kennelly was an Irishman from Bridgeport. Born in 1887, he grew up poor. He graduated from De La Salle Institute, then worked in a warehouse before serving as a captain in the U.S. Army Quartermaster Corps during World War I. Mustered out in 1919, he started a business hauling furniture.

Kennelly prospered. Within a few years he had one of the largest moving and storage companies in the city. His financial success allowed him to leave

"He looked like a statesman!" Mayor Martin Kennelly. *Author's collection.*

the old neighborhood behind in favor of a posh lakefront apartment. A lifelong bachelor, he shared the flat with a widowed sister.

He also dabbled in local Democratic politics as a contributor. Kennelly supported various candidates from the party's reform wing, some of them successful, some of them not. The party regulars had enough respect for Kennelly's stalwart public image—and for the depth of his wallet—to overlook his embrace of independent-minded mavericks. He was twice offered organization backing for elective office but refused. He did, however, accept an appointment to the Chicago Park District Board.

The situation changed in 1947, when Edward J. Kelly was finishing up fourteen years as mayor. There had been a series of scandals, and the Republicans looked like they had a shot at reclaiming the mayor's chair. Remember, this was back in 1947.

The party mandarins told Kelly it was time to retire. Kennelly was a popular civic leader with no political taint; he was the perfect "clean" candidate for mayor. This time he agreed to run, with the understanding that there would be no strings attached. "We must get away from the idea that government belongs to a party and realize it belongs to the people," he told party slate makers. "I do not subscribe to the principle of 'to the victor belong the spoils.'"

Kennelly really meant it, and the Democratic pols knew he meant it. They were so desperate that they were willing to go along with him. Though the Republicans did pick up eighteen of the fifty city council seats, Kennelly was elected mayor.

Chicago was enjoying a postwar boom. Kennelly's tenure saw many major public works projects, including the Congress (Eisenhower) Expressway, O'Hare Airport, the Milwaukee-Dearborn subway, and the extensions of both Lake Shore Drive and Wacker Drive. After two decades of depression and war, private construction also rebounded.

Kennelly worked to clean up the public school system and had some success. His efforts to reform civil service had less of an impact. His raids on open gambling generated a lot of newspaper ink—and brought him political trouble.

Most of Kennelly's gambling raids took place in the South Side fief of Congressman William L. Dawson. Dawson and his constituents were African American, and he saw the mayor's actions as racist. Calls for party unity finally convinced Dawson to support Kennelly for reelection in 1951.

Kennelly won that 1951 election without much bother. Still, party leaders had decided the mayor was a loose cannon. He had to be replaced the next time around.

Cook County clerk Richard J. Daley became the Democratic chairman in 1953. Two years later, when Kennelly appeared before the party slate makers to ask for their endorsement, he was dumbfounded when they picked Daley instead. Embarrassed and angry, he ran against Daley in the mayoral primary.

Kennelly had never shown much enthusiasm for personal politicking. Now he mounted a vigorous campaign. But he was finally learning to say "hello" when it was time to say "goodbye." Daley won the primary and then the general election.

Kennelly retired to his Sheridan Road apartment, and little was heard from him from then on. He died in 1961. Years later, one scholar began an essay on Kennelly's political career with a simple sentence that might serve as his epitaph: "He was a nice man."

# THE SULLIVAN OF SULLIVAN HIGH SCHOOL

Roger Sullivan wasn't an educator, or a scientist, or an explorer, or a military hero, or a celebrated humanitarian. His public service consisted of a single term as a probate court clerk. So, why does he have a high school named after him?

In Chicago, the reason is obvious. Roger Sullivan was the political boss who built the Democratic machine.

Sullivan grew up in rural poverty outside Belvidere, where he'd been born in 1861. He came to Chicago as a teenager to work in the West Side railyards, and soon got involved in politics. His election to the Cook County Probate Court came in 1890.

Chicago had a competitive, two-party system then. The Democrats had several factions that battled among themselves. The Republicans were divided that way, too. If either party could become united, that party would easily win elections. Different political chieftains kept trying to build a permanent coalition. Sullivan was the man who succeeded.

Beginning around 1900, Sullivan started working to bring local Democrats together. Often it was like herding cats. His main nemesis was on-and-off mayor Carter Harrison Jr. Harrison liked to don the cloak of respectability, claiming that Sullivan was nothing more than a corrupt wheeler-dealer, though Harrison saw nothing wrong about his own alliance with such notorious public servants as Hinky Dink Kenna and Bathhouse John Coughlin. For his part, Sullivan refused to stoop to personal attacks, instead keeping his focus on the main goal.

In 1910 Sullivan managed to unite all the party factions behind a "harmony ticket" for the fall elections. The emerging ethnic blocs were not ignored. In putting together the ticket, it was expressly stated that the candidates for certain key offices were "to be named by the Poles," or "to be named by the Bohemians," and so on. Though the fragile unity collapsed soon after the election, more and more local Democrats were seeing the wisdom of a consolidated party organization. They continued to move into the Sullivan camp.

Meanwhile, Sullivan was also becoming a force in national politics. He had been elected Democratic National Committeeman from Illinois in 1906. At the tumultuous 1912 convention, he helped break a deadlock and secure the nomination for Woodrow Wilson, who went on to win the presidency. Once safely in office, the new president did little to acknowledge Sullivan's help. Secretary of State William Jennings Bryan was Sullivan's sworn enemy.

Chicago remembers Roger Sullivan. *Photograph by the author.*

Besides, the Chicago man looked to be just the sort of sleazy politico Wilson had battled in New Jersey.

That last characterization was doing Roger Sullivan a disservice. Later historians have recognized him as a backroom boss who had the vision to work for progressive causes. He supported women's suffrage, direct primaries, and other reform measures. Long before Richard J. Daley popularized the slogan, Sullivan believed that good government could be good politics.

Sullivan himself became quite wealthy. His enemies made pointed hints about how he'd obtained that wealth—there were a couple of controversial utilities deals—but nothing illegal was ever proven. There was enough money to be made from politics in legal ways without blatant stealing from the public treasury.

In 1914, after decades operating behind the scenes, Sullivan became a candidate for the United States Senate. "The Chief wants to be a statesman," one of his associates explained. Illinois was still a Republican state, and Sullivan lost, but only by 17,000 votes.

He went back to building the local party. By 1920 Harrison and the other factional leaders had been defeated, and Sullivan had control centralized in his hands. Newspapers were starting to write about the Democratic "machine." His work completed, Sullivan talked about retiring after the fall elections. Then, on April 14, he died of a heart attack.

He had played hardball politics but had never been vindictive. "The checkerboard is moving all the time," he once said. "The men who are strong enemies today may be friendly six months from now." In his obituary, the Republican *Tribune* called Sullivan "the benevolent boss" of Illinois Democrats.

In 1926 the Roger Sullivan Junior High School opened at 6631 North Bosworth Avenue. When the city later abolished junior highs, it became a four-year general high school, as it remains today.

# A Tale of Two Kellys

Politicians love to get their names on things. Besides being a campaign asset, it is a bit of immortality. So, when a politician passes on, it's natural that the living politicians try to find something public that they can name to honor a departed colleague.

In Chicago, this process can become convoluted. Take Kelly High School and Kelly Park, for example. They are both Southwest Side institutions located across California Avenue from one another, just south of Archer Avenue. But each of them is named for a different Kelly.

Thomas Kelly is the earlier and more obscure Kelly. He was born in Rhode Island in 1843, grew up on a farm in Wisconsin, and came to Chicago in 1861, poor but ambitious. Tom Kelly worked in a grocery store and for a meatpacker. In 1876 he moved to suburban Brighton Park to manage a cotton mill. Later he went into the real estate business.

Kelly became active in the Democratic Party after Brighton Park was annexed by Chicago in 1889. Over the next two decades, he always seemed to hold a public office. Kelly was a member of the Chicago Board of Education, served two terms as Twenty-Eighth Ward alderman, then was elected president of the Chicago Sanitary District. In 1912 he was once again appointed to the school board. When he died two years later, the entire board attended his funeral.

In 1928 the city opened a new junior high school at 4136 South California Avenue. Since Tom Kelly had been on the school board and had lived in the neighborhood, the building was named for him. Junior high schools were eliminated in 1933, and Tom Kelly's school became a four-year high school.

Kelly High School also owned a parcel of vacant land across the street, on the east side of California. In 1947 the Chicago Park District signed a lease for the property with the idea of building a park. A number of adjacent homeowners were forced to sell by court order, and their houses were leveled. Kelly Park was dedicated on the property in 1951.

Now we turn our attention to the other Kelly. Edward Joseph Kelly was not related to Thomas Kelly. This particular Kelly was a native Chicagoan, born in 1876 and raised in Bridgeport. At eighteen he got a job as a laborer for the Sanitary District. Hardworking, smart, and tough, he moved up in the ranks. He also got into Democratic politics. That eventually led to his appointment as the district's chief engineer.

By 1933 Ed Kelly had become president of the South Parks Commission. Then Mayor Anton Cermak was assassinated. The law said that Cermak's successor had to be chosen from among the sitting aldermen. But after some fancy maneuvering, Kelly wound up as mayor. He served until 1947, the longest tenure in the city's history at that point. His administration was not noted for its efficiency or its high ethical standards.

The retired mayor died on October 20, 1950. Today, the signs at the park across from the high school read "Edward J. Kelly Park, established 1951." However, it is not clear when Ed Kelly's name was actually given to the park.

Looking across Kelly Park toward Kelly High School. *Photograph by the author.*

I had an older friend who grew up nearby. He said that the vacant land on the east side of California Avenue was informally called "Kelly Park" as early as the 1930s. School athletic teams practiced there, and it was considered an integral part of the Kelly High School campus.

Maybe the Ed Kelly dedication did take place in 1951. Maybe it took place in 1991, when the board of education transferred its portion of the property to the Park District. Maybe it happened sometime in between. The end result is a sort of cut-rate commemoration, two politicians for the price of one.

In any event, like Tom Kelly, Ed Kelly now has his own bit of immortality. And as much as any local politician, he deserves to be remembered. After all, he is still the longest-serving Chicago mayor whose name is not Daley.

# A TALE OF TWO TOMBS

People go into politics for various reasons. Perhaps it is to do good, or to wield power, or to get rich, or for any combination of the above, or maybe for something entirely different. However, there is one motivation that drives nearly all politicians.

They want to be famous. And that doesn't stop when death intrudes. Consider two Chicago politicians who are separated by over a century but united in their desire to be remembered.

John Wentworth came to Chicago as a twenty-one-year-old in 1836. Nicknamed "Long John" because he was six foot six, he carried on a law practice, speculated in real estate, and published a newspaper. He started his political career as a Democrat, then switched to the antislavery Republican Party.

Wentworth served twelve years in the U.S. House of Representatives. However, it was his two terms as the mayor of Chicago that got Wentworth a major street named in his honor. He was a "hands-on" executive, pulling down overhead signs that obstructed the sidewalks and leading raids on the city's vice district. He even personally put his hands on a lawyer and forcibly ejected him from a prison. When the young prince of Wales visited the city in 1860, Chicago's mayor decided to show the royal visitor a real American saloon. "Boys," he told the gathered patrons in a loud voice, "this is the prince. Prince, these are the boys."

Wentworth spent his later years living on a large estate in the outskirts of the city, near Archer and Harlem Avenues. In 1886 he began building his tomb in Rosehill Cemetery. At a cost of $38,000 Long John had a fifty-ton granite obelisk fashioned in New Hampshire, then hauled to Chicago by train, boat, and wagon. After it was set on its base over the gravesite, the pillar was seventy-two feet high, taller than anything else on the property, and clearly visible from Peterson Avenue.

Wentworth gave instructions that nothing should be inscribed on the obelisk or its base—not even his name. When asked for an explanation, he said, "People will ask whose monument it is. When informed it is John Wentworth's monument, they will ransack old records and visit libraries to find out who John Wentworth was. When they find out, they will remember."

Wentworth died in 1888. His heirs put his name on the monument anyway.

Roland Burris was born in 1937 in downstate Centralia. As an African American growing up in the mid-twentieth century, he overcame many obstacles and became a successful commercial lawyer. He was elected to three terms as the Illinois comptroller and a single term as the state's attorney general.

In December 2008, Governor Rod Blagojevich appointed Burris to the U.S. Senate seat being vacated by president-elect Barack Obama. Blagojevich was later convicted of trying to sell that appointment, but Burris had no part in the scheme. The Senate seated him, and he served there for just under two years.

Roland Burris celebrated his eighty-third birthday in August 2020. Like John Wentworth, he has paid careful attention to his final resting place. Unlike Long John, Burris has rejected the minimalist approach.

The Burris Tomb is located in the northwest section of Oak Woods Cemetery, prominently sited at the junction of two driveways. On the central granite slab, under the heading "Trail Blazer," the inscription says Burris was the first African American in Illinois to serve as comptroller, the first to serve as attorney general, the first to be a Southern Illinois University exchange student to Hamburg University in Germany, the first to be a national bank examiner, the first to be elected president of the National Association of State Auditors, Comptrollers, and Treasurers—and so on.

The two side panels list Burris's other "Major Accomplishments," such as being the vice-chairman of the Democratic National Committee. At the time of this writing, there is no mention of the U.S. Senate on the tomb.

John Wentworth wanted to be remembered and could trust in the curiosity of future generations. In our time, Roland Burris has had to spell everything

The prospective tomb of Roland Burris in Oak Woods Cemetery. *Photograph by the author.*

out. Somewhere in these companion stories, there's the seed of a scholarly monograph on the decline of American education.

# BATHHOUSE JOHN

*Was there ever really a Bathhouse John Coughlin? Did such a man truly stalk the corridors of the Chicago City Hall? Wasn't he just a character of fiction, created by a fanciful journalist or scriptwriter as a symbol of every crooked-but-colorful ward politician in history?*

Banish your doubts. Yes, Virginia—and yes, Virgil—there really was a Bathhouse John.

John Joseph Coughlin was born in Chicago in 1860. His boyhood home was in the First Ward, near Wells and Polk Streets, where his Irish immigrant father owned a grocery store. Young Johnny grew up tall, strong, friendly, and not very bright. He ambled through a series of jobs that depended more on brawn than brain. One of these jobs was giving postshower rubdowns to patrons at a Clark Street Bathhouse. From that time on, he was known as Bathhouse John—or simply the Bath.

Along the way he got into politics. Soon he was moving up in the First Ward Democratic organization. Coughlin was an entertaining public speaker, and he didn't ask questions. That qualified him to be elected alderman in 1892.

Chicago then had thirty-five wards, with two aldermen from each. Coughlin's longtime colleague was Michael Kenna, who was known as Hinky Dink because he was small. Coughlin had the charm, and Kenna had the brains. Together, they made an effective team.

They were effective in bringing in votes, that is. Besides taking in the Loop, the First Ward stretched down past Twenty-Second Street (Cermak Road) and included most of the city's gambling halls and brothels. These businesses were technically illegal, so the operators paid bribes to operate.

By the turn of the twentieth century, Coughlin represented everything the clean government crowd hated. He was basically a good-natured man with little interest in textbook theory whose attitude was "live and let live." He answered the reformers' scorn with cheerful bluster. That just made them angrier.

Reporters loved Coughlin, because he made for good copy. If there wasn't much news on a particular day, the Bath could be counted on for a story. The city's nine dailies were always quoting one of outrageous pronouncements or detailing his latest brainstorm as serious matters to be pondered by concerned citizens.

One example of this was his Dress Reform Movement. The Bath had decided that men's clothing was too dull, so he began appearing at council meetings in a bright green suit. A friend told him that he looked like "an Evanston lawn kissed by the morning dew," and that encouraged Coughlin to try even gaudier costumes. His most bizarre outfit combined a blue-and-white flannel coat, a yellow vest with orange spots, and brown-and-white checked trousers.

Bathhouse John Coughlin shows off his latest raiment. *From the* Chicago Tribune, *December 22, 1908.*

Coughlin was also a writer. He composed a ballad titled "Dear Midnight of Love," which was performed at the opera house by a brass band and a chorus of fifty. His poetry included such works as "She Sleeps by the Drainage Canal," "They're Tearing Up Clark Street Again" and "Ode to a Bathtub." A reporter later admitted he had helped the alderman with his literary output.

The Bath's ambitions never went beyond the First Ward. He always "stuck to the small stuff." Coughlin and Kenna ruled their little fief, pocketed their money, and delivered votes to the candidate who offered the best deal. The party went on unchanged for three decades.

In 1923 the Chicago ward system was restructured to the current fifty wards, with one alderman from each. Kenna stepped aside so Coughlin could keep the spotlight. By that time it was all show. Control of the First Ward had passed to Al Capone. Since the Bath didn't pose any threat, Capone allowed him to continue on as before.

Coughlin grew older and fatter. His fortune trickled away. He attended council meetings but seldom spoke. He had become a living souvenir of a wild and woolly past, like the crazy uncle who is tolerated in his dotage. Even his old nemesis the *Tribune* now published nostalgic articles about the once-notorious First Ward Ball.

He died on November 8, 1938, leaving behind debts of $56,000 and a string of lethargic racehorses. The city council draped its chambers in mourning. And in the front row, at the desk John Coughlin had occupied for forty-six years, someone placed a bowl of roses.

## 4.

# SPORTS AND SPORTSMEN

## CAP ANSON

His life sounded like the plot of a dime novel from the turn of the twentieth century. He was born in a log cabin in Iowa in 1852 and grew up in a little farm settlement called Marshalltown. At nineteen he set out for the big city to earn his fortune. He worked hard at his profession, got rich, and became a leading citizen of Chicago and one of the most famous men in the country.

His name was Adrian Constantine Anson. He was a baseball player.

Professional baseball was a risky career choice when Anson started playing. The pay was low, and teams often folded. After a season at Rockford and four more at Philadelphia, Anson signed on with the Chicago White Stockings in the new National League in 1876.

He was a big man for his time, standing at six foot one and weighing 220 pounds. With Chicago he usually played first base. In 1879 he took over as the team's captain-manager and soon became known as Cap Anson. Then the legend began.

During the 1880s he established himself as baseball's number-one player. The game was indeed becoming a national pastime, with Anson becoming a national hero—"his name was better known than any soldier or statesman of his time," one historian wrote. Fans hung his portrait on their walls, kept scrapbooks of his achievements, and proudly wore hats emblazoned with his name. People who had never met him named newborn babies "Anson."

His White Stockings—the lineal ancestor of today's Cubs—won five National League Championships. Anson was the first player to collect a career total of three thousand hits. In an era when home runs were rare, he once hit five of them over the course of two games, a feat that wasn't duplicated for over forty years. In 1939 he became one of the first players elected to the Baseball Hall of Fame.

Despite all of this, he left baseball with one negative legacy. Anson refused to play against African Americans. In an 1884 exhibition game, he threatened to take the White Stockings off the field unless Toledo removed its Black catcher. The Toledo manager refused the demand, and Anson played anyway. Over the next few years, there were at least two other incidents in which Anson did succeed in bullying the opposition into benching a Black player.

Anson was probably no more racist than most White Americans of his time. But he was also baseball's leading player. His example prompted the sport to adopt an informal "color line," which lasted until 1945.

Anson retired from active play in 1897. The next year he opened a combination billiard hall and bowling alley in the Loop known as Anson's Emporium. It soon became a local hangout for the sporting crowd and a major tourist attraction. Anson himself was an expert bowler. In 1904 he took a team to the American Bowling Congress Tournament in Cleveland and came home with the first-place trophy. That made him the answer to a famous sports trivia question: "Who is the only man elected to the Baseball Hall of Fame who also won a national bowling championship?"

Fresh from his bowling triumph, Anson entered politics. In 1905 he was elected Chicago city clerk as a Democrat. But within a few years, everything came crashing down.

Anson had traded on his fame to become city clerk. That proved to be his limit. He ran for Cook County sheriff in 1906 and lost in the primary. The next year he was defeated in his reelection bid as clerk. His Emporium went bankrupt in 1909. As a businessman and as a politician, Cap Anson was one helluva baseball player.

Cap Anson, looking dignified as a candidate for Chicago City Clerk. *Author's collection.*

He was broke. Today he might support himself autographing baseballs or working as a casino greeter. In Anson's time, his best option was the vaudeville stage. His friends Ring Lardner and George M. Cohan helped Anson put together a monologue, and for several years, he toured with two of his daughters.

Cap Anson died in 1922. He was buried in Oak Woods Cemetery. The graveyard later became the final resting place of Jesse Owens, Harold Washington, and other prominent African Americans. But if Anson had any objection to this form of integration, he has not been heard from.

# MAN OF STEEL

Everybody who knew Tony Zale said he was one of the nicest men they'd ever met. That was Tony Zale the man. Tony Zale the boxer was something different. "It was like Jekyll and Hyde," one observer said. "Once he got in the ring, he was Mr. Hyde."

He was born Anthony Florian Zaleski in Gary in 1913. His father worked in the steel mills until he was killed in an accident when Tony was two. Mrs. Zaleski, who was eight months pregnant when her husband died, went to work scrubbing floors after the baby was born.

As soon as they were old enough, Tony and his two older brothers got jobs in the mills. Tony also did some amateur boxing on the side. In 1934 he turned pro as a middleweight. Like Joe Louis around the same time, Tony changed his name so his mother wouldn't know what he was doing.

Zale honed his craft the hard way. For six years he fought in small Chicago arenas, mostly winning but also losing, while getting banged up in the process. Then he broke through.

In July 1940 Zale beat Al Hostak to win a share of the disputed middleweight championship. The other claimant was Georgie Adams, and it took over a year to get both men into the same ring. They finally fought on November 28, 1941. Zale won and became undisputed champ. Nine days later, America was plunged into World War II.

Zale enlisted in the navy. He kept his title for the duration but didn't have a chance to make money from it. By the time the war ended in 1945, he was thirty-two and thought to be past his prime.

Now the big-name middleweight was Rocky Graziano. He'd served jail time and later had been thrown out of the army with a dishonorable discharge. After that he turned to boxing, winning a string of wartime victories.

Zale faced off against Graziano in September 1946. The challenger was six years younger than the champ and a two-to-one favorite. For five rounds, Graziano pounded Zale. In the sixth round, the referee was about to stop the slaughter when Zale called on his last bit of strength and knocked out Graziano.

Boxing writers called the bout one of the most exciting in history. There had to be a rematch! So, in July 1947, they went at it again. This time, Zale clobbered Graziano for five rounds. And this time, Graziano came back to win in the sixth round, taking the middleweight crown.

Again the experts labeled the fight one of boxing's greatest. Again there were cries for a rematch.

Zale-Graziano III went off in June 1948. Zale was closing in on his thirty-fifth birthday; he was just in the ring to grab a paycheck and couldn't possibly come back. At least, that was the narrative until Zale floored Graziano in the third round and regained the middleweight crown.

The writers were calling Zale the Man of Steel. Though the nickname referred to his work in the Gary mills, it was also the nickname of Superman. Yet even Tony Zale had to face the reality of the calendar. Three months after the third Graziano bout, Marcel Cerdan stopped him in the twelfth round. Now Zale hung up his gloves for good.

He tried a number of things in retirement. He had a restaurant for a while. Later he had the Tony Zale Insurance Agency. He put his name on magazine articles. He coached boxing.

Meanwhile, Graziano—the man he'd whipped in two out of three bouts—was getting rich as an entertainer and "personality." Zale asked a sportswriter for advice on how to cash in. "Go put the screws on somebody, and you'll make money," the writer said. Zale, always the gentleman, said no.

In 1958 Zale made a cameo appearance as himself in a movie about Graziano. Later there was another movie about another controversial middleweight from his era, Jake La Motta.

It's unlikely there will ever be a movie about Tony Zale. He was too much of a straight arrow. But a few years before his 1997 death, he received the Presidential Citizens Medal from President George H. Bush. That has to count for something.

# CHICAGO'S FORGOTTEN BASEBALL TEAM

In the early twentieth century, America's cities were growing. Baseball was popular. The country already had the National and American Leagues. Surely there was room for a third major league.

In 1913 a group of entrepreneurs organized the Federal League. At first the new league did nothing to challenge the National and American Leagues' monopoly. The Chicago team, known as the Chifeds, was headed by local businessman James A. Gilmore and played its games at De Paul University's baseball diamond. Operating on a tight budget, the Federal League got through the 1913 season.

Now the league began attracting some deep-pocket investors. For 1914 the Feds declared themselves a full-fledged major league. They immediately began trying to sign players away from the two established majors. Gilmore was named the new league president. That opened the door for Charlie Weeghman.

Weeghman had made his money running a string of low-cost lunch counters around Chicago. A few years earlier, he'd been rebuffed in a bid to buy the St. Louis Cardinals. Taking over the Chicago Federal League franchise, he immediately began operating.

"Going Major" meant the Chifeds needed a first-class ballpark. With the White Sox playing on the South Side and the Cubs on the West Side, Weeghman staked out territory on the North Side. In December 1913 he secured a ninety-nine-year lease on a parcel of land at Clark and Addison Streets. He hired Zachary Taylor Davis, the architect of Comiskey Park, to design the new Weeghman Field. Work began erecting the steel-and-concrete stadium.

That same month, Weeghman pulled off a coup by signing Joe Tinker as the Chifeds manager and shortstop. The onetime Cubs star was the first "name" player to throw in his lot with the new circuit. Tinker's signing gave notice that the Feds meant business. Over that winter, a bidding war broke out as the Feds tried to entice more players into their camp.

The Chifeds opened their new stadium on April 24, 1914. A capacity crowd of over eighteen thousand people was on hand. Bands played, schoolchildren marched, and the ladies' auxiliary of the Grand Army of the Republic displayed a giant American flag. The home team capped the day with a 9–1 victory over the Kansas City Packers.

Throughout the season, the Feds fought the National and American Leagues' monopoly in the courts. On the field, the new league held its

The Cubs and the Sox refuse to play the Federal League's Chicago Whales. *From the* Chicago Tribune, *September 21, 1915.*

own. In Chicago and other cities where they faced off against the older leagues, the Feds cut heavily into ballpark patronage. Federal League owners said they were willing to put up with a few seasons of red ink. They were playing a long game.

In Chicago, the Cubs and Sox were having mediocre seasons. Meanwhile, the Chifeds were battling for the league pennant. The 1914 season ended with the team in second place, only one game behind the champion Indianapolis Hoosiers. Pitcher Claude Hendrix led the league with twenty-nine wins.

In 1915 the Chifeds were given a new name: the Chicago Whales. But the big news came when the team announced it had signed the great Walter Johnson of the Washington Senators. Alarmed that baseball's best pitcher would be drawing more fans away from his team, Sox owner Charles Comiskey quietly paid Johnson $10,000 to stay in Washington.

The renamed Whales opened their season before another capacity crowd on April 10. Newly elected mayor William Hale Thompson threw out the ceremonial first pitch. Once again, the team was in the thick of the pennant race. But some of the Federal League owners were growing tired of the baseball war. Peace talks with the two established leagues began.

The 1915 Federal League pennant race turned out to be one of the closest in all major league history. The Whales squeezed out the championship over

St. Louis and Pittsburgh. Spitball ace Slats McConnell topped the league's pitchers with twenty-five victories.

That December, the Feds signed a peace treaty with the two older major leagues. The Federal League was dissolved. Weeghman bought a controlling interest in the Cubs, bringing with him Tinker, McConnell, Hendrix, and the best Whales players. He also moved the Cubs to the ballpark at Clark and Addison, where they remain to this day.

## A WINNING CHICAGO ATHLETE

Chicago sports have long had the reputation for producing lovable losers. Johnny Weissmuller was different. He was a swimmer. And he never lost.

There always was controversy over where and when Johnny was born. Although he may have been born in Pennsylvania in any one of several different years, the best guess is that Johann Peter Weissmuller was born in the village of Freisdorf in what's now Romania in 1904. Wherever he came from, Johnny spent a good chunk of his childhood in Chicago.

He grew up in the old German neighborhood near North Avenue and Larrabee Street. Johnny was a sickly kid, so the family doctor suggested he take up some sport to improve his health. He went out for the high jump at school and was rotten at it. Then the doctor told him to try swimming. That would make all the difference.

Johnny went to Lane Tech for a short time—it was close to his home on Sedgwick Street then—but dropped out. He drifted through a number of jobs. His big break came when he was fifteen and working as an elevator operator.

One day he appeared at the Illinois Athletic Club and asked to try out for the swim team. The coach told him to swim the length of the pool and back. Johnny's style was unpolished and raw. But the coach saw that the kid had potential and agreed to work with him.

For the next year, Johnny trained religiously. One story says that he supplemented his routine at the club by swimming laps around Goose Island in the Chicago River. He also picked up some extra cash by boxing under an assumed name at North Side fight clubs. That lasted until another boxer knocked him out cold.

After that year of training, the club swim coach decided Johnny was ready for competition. He took the sixteen-year-old kid to the 1921 Amateur Athletic Union Championships in Minnesota. Though Johnny was only a rookie, he won every event he entered with ease. Over the next few years, each swim meet was the same thing—Weissmuller against the field. The field always came in second.

He set speed records, broke them, then broke them again. At the 1924 Olympics he won three gold medals and shared a bronze as a member of a water polo team. In the process, he outraced the legendary Duke Kahanamoku, recognized for years as the world's greatest swimmer.

But that honor belonged to Johnny Weissmuller now. Back home, Johnny continued winning every competition he entered. He became one of the sports demigods of the Roaring Twenties, often mentioned in the same breath as Babe Ruth, Jack Dempsey, Red Grange and the rest. Bookies stopped taking bets on his races. The only action they'd accept was on how much time Johnny might shave off his latest world record.

He was at the Olympics again in 1928. Entering two freestyle events, Johnny claimed two more golds. By then he had won fifty-two amateur championships and set sixty-seven different records. He'd never been beaten in formal competition. With nothing left to prove, he retired from swimming.

The scrawny teen had built himself into a six-foot-four hunk. For a while Johnny modeled for a bathing suit company. Then, in 1932, he went to Hollywood to star in the movie *Tarzan the Ape Man*. The film was an unexpected hit, and Weissmuller went on to make a dozen Tarzan epics.

He was a terrible actor, and he knew it. Still, being Tarzan did have its perks. In 1958, years after his last movie, Weissmuller was at a golf outing in Cuba when his party was suddenly captured by rifle-toting rebels. Johnny got out of his car, stood tall, and smiled at the men surrounding him. Then he let loose his famous movie jungle yell. With that, the rebels lowered their rifles, smiled back, and began calling out, "Tarzan! Tarzan!" They then gave Johnny an armed escort back to his hotel.

Johnny went through five wives and a lot of money in his life, but he never lost his charm or sense of humor. In his later years, he wound up in the traditional sinecure of the down-and-out athlete, working as a greeter in a Las Vegas casino. He died in 1984.

# BOWLER OF THE HALF-CENTURY

When bowling was big and when Chicago was the bowling capital of the world, the greatest bowler in Chicago was Paul Krumske. And there is one story about Paul Krumske they always tell.

During a close match, Krumske suddenly keels over on the lane, grabbing his chest and gasping for breath. The match stops. Medical help is summoned, and Krumske is revived. He gamely declares that he will go on. By now the opposition is totally unnerved—especially when Krumske rolls the next half-dozen strikes

This incident happened during the famous match Krumske bowled against Ned Day...in a team match in the Chicago Classic League...in a tournament in Detroit...in a late-night pot game at Faetz-Niesen. Maybe he faked heart attacks on all those occasions. After the first few times, though, you'd think the other bowlers would get wise and just step over Paul as they bowled.

Born on the South Side in 1912, Krumske dropped out of high school to go to work as a clerk at a meatpacking plant. One evening, when he was seventeen, the boss needed a sub on his bowling team. Krumske volunteered.

He learned fast. Within five years of picking up a bowling ball, Krumske had rolled a 300 game and was carrying one of the highest averages in the city. The sports pages began running stories about the new boy wonder of Chicago bowling.

There wasn't any professional bowling then. The better bowlers all had day jobs. They made extra money by getting on a top-flight team and competing in leagues and tournaments. Bowlers who were really good might attract some deep-pocket backers who'd stake them in matches against other hotshots, paying them a percentage of any winnings.

Krumske followed these career routes. He bowled in the city's top league, the Chicago Classic, for nearly forty years. For twenty years, he was league secretary. Recognized as one of the country's top players, he was named to the annual All-American Team seven times.

Krumske's finest moment came in 1944. Ned Day was bowling's match-game champion—the equivalent of boxing's heavyweight champ. He'd never been beaten in a head-to-head match. Krumske wanted to bowl the champ, but his financial angels were wary of putting any cash in such a risky venture. Krumske finally managed to scrape together $1,000 to seal the match. Then he went out and beat Day for the title in an eighty-game showdown.

In 1951 a newspaper poll named Krumske Chicago's Bowler of the Half-Century. Bowling was starting to enjoy a boom era. By now Krumske was endorsing bowling products and giving exhibitions for an equipment manufacturer. One local bowling alley employed him as a part-time instructor on the weekend.

Jerry Lewis mugs with Paul Krumske before their televised match. *Courtesy of the* Bowlers Journal.

He also had a full-time job at the Peter Hand Brewery. His title there was sports director. In this position, Krumske was captain of the brewery's famed Meister Brau Beer bowling team. By staying in the news, the team helped sell beer. And as secretary of the Chicago Classic, Krumske could convince bowling proprietors to stock Meister Brau in their bars.

Krumske appeared on the many bowling shows that were popular in the early days of television. For a while he had his own program called *Bowl the Professor*. The format of the half-hour show had Krumske giving bowling tips while rolling a one-game match against a local amateur.

In 1957 comedian Jerry Lewis made a surprise appearance on the show. His hilarious match against Krumske was taped and used in fundraising for Lewis's favorite charity, the Muscular Dystrophy Association. The tape was so successful that a Lewis-Krumske "rematch" was later staged, taped, and distributed as well.

Like most athletes, Krumske's skills declined as he grew older. His bowling winnings shrank. His exhibition contract was not renewed. Then, in 1972, the brewery closed.

Krumske did some instructing and ran a few tournaments. Early in 1979, he decided to make a fresh start and moved to Florida. That same summer, Paul Krumske died in his new Boca Raton home.

The cause of death was a heart attack.

# Chicago's Forgotten Football Team

The year was 1946. World War II had ended, and golden times were ahead. Though baseball was still the national pastime, football was the up-and-coming sport. *Chicago Tribune* sports editor Arch Ward was convinced there was room for a second professional league to challenge the established National Football League. He eventually found enough interested investors to launch a new eight-team league called the All-America Football Conference (AAFC).

The Chicago franchise in the new league was awarded to Jack Keeshin, a trucking executive who'd failed in a bid to buy the White Sox. The city already had two National Football League (NFL) teams, the Bears and the Cardinals. But the Cardinals were underfinanced and had been forced to merge with the Pittsburgh Steelers during the war. Keeshin thought he could drive them out of town.

Keeshin named his team the Rockets. That word had been in the news a lot during the final days of the war, as the German V-2 rockets had rained destruction on Great Britain. A rocket represented the latest innovation in science. It was also something powerful and deadly.

Naturally, Ward's *Tribune* gave the AAFC wide publicity. Stories were leaked that the Rockets would sign Sid Luckman and other Bears stars. The team announced it would play in Soldier Field, which wasn't being used for much of anything in 1946 and had 100,000 seats to accommodate the expected crowds. With the season opener a month away, Ward reported that "advance sale of season tickets for the Chicago Rockets home games has passed $100,000, the heaviest demand in the history of Chicago football."

Then things began to go wrong for the Rockets. In a preseason practice, rookie halfback Bill McArthur fractured his leg. Complications developed, and the leg had to be amputated. Meanwhile, most of the top-level players preferred to stick with the NFL. The Rockets were unable to recruit any big names.

The Rockets opened at home against the Cleveland Browns on September 13 and lost, 20–6. After a tie the next week, the team ran off two straight wins, before descending into mediocrity. The season ended with the Rockets at the bottom of the AAFC Western Division, with a record of 5–6–3. Despite Ward's preseason hype, both the Bears and Cardinals outdrew the Rockets.

Trying to find a winning formula, Jack Keeshin had gone through five head coaches. At the end of the season, he bailed. AAFC commissioner Jim Crowley stepped down and took over as the head of a new ownership group.

The 1947 Rockets were even worse than they had been the previous season. They lost their first ten games, eked out a victory, then dropped three more for a 1–13 record and another basement finish. Meanwhile, across town, the Cardinals won the NFL Championship. Even if the Rockets had fielded a super team, they wouldn't be driving out the Cardinals any time soon.

As the team sputtered along, Ward tried a desperate maneuver. He secretly met with Coach Paul Brown of the Cleveland Browns and suggested they trade star quarterback Otto Graham to the Rockets. Graham was a Waukegan boy who'd played college football at Northwestern, and Ward thought he would be a huge gate attraction in Chicago. Brown turned down the plan.

The Rockets continued their losing ways in 1948, with another 1–13 record and their customary spot at the bottom of the standings. On September 26, halfback Elroy "Crazylegs" Hirsch was kicked in the head during a game, putting him out of action with a fractured skull. Hirsch was the team's one marquee player. With Crazylegs gone, there was little reason left for fans to freeze at Soldier Field while watching the Rockets lose.

Aiming for a fresh start in 1949, the team changed its name to the Chicago Hornets. Maybe they thought they could cash in on the popularity of the *Green Hornet* comic strip. NFL legend Ray Flaherty took over as head coach. The team's record improved to 4–8, and they finally managed to escape last place.

After the season was over, the NFL and AAFC ended their war. Three AAFC teams were admitted to the NFL, but the Chicago Hornets (also known as the Rockets) did not survive. The team was disbanded, and its players were dispersed to the remaining professional teams.

## GODFATHER OF BIG-BUCKS GOLF

George S. May was never much of a golfer. When he broke 100, he would celebrate for a week. Yet as much as anyone, he paved the way for golf to become a multimillion-dollar sport.

Born on a downstate Illinois farm in 1890, May graduated from a state teachers' college, then decided he wanted to do something else with his life. His first adult job was as a traveling Bible salesman. He finally settled on a career as an efficiency expert, and in 1925 started his own consulting firm. Though the Great Depression killed many businesses, May prospered. By the late 1930s, he was a millionaire.

Meanwhile, May had been buying shares in the moribund Tam O'Shanter Golf Club in Niles. He eventually acquired a controlling interest. In 1940 he went to the U.S. Open in Cleveland as a spectator. That trip convinced him that he could do a better job running a golf tournament.

May's first All-American Open was held at Tam O'Shanter in the summer of 1941. The total purse was $11,000, the richest on the Professional Golfers' Association Tour. Yet at the same time, May slashed ticket prices to $1.00 and offered free parking as well.

The gallery at golf tournaments had always been limited to a few hundred hardcore cognoscenti. May was aiming at volume sales. He advertised lavishly, with full-page newspaper advertisements and thirty-second radio commercials. Even if people had no interest in golf, they could still enjoy a relaxing day in the country at beautiful Tam O'Shanter.

May's plan worked. More than forty thousand people showed up for the tournament's first four days, with another twenty-three thousand on hand for the final round on Sunday.

May kept his All-American Open going throughout World War II, paying prizes in war bonds and donating profits to the Army Emergency Relief Fund. He also added a women's professional tournament and an amateur event. And with tire rationing cutting down automobile travel, he refunded the fares of spectators who came by public transit.

After the war ended in 1945, May really got going. He launched another tournament called the World's Championship. Spectator grandstands were erected at select holes, with shortwave radio reports piped in from other parts of the course. The clubhouse swimming pool was opened to the public. Evening dances were held on the outdoor pavilion. Cash prizes were awarded to lucky ticket holders. Automobiles were raffled off next to the practice green.

Golf traditionalists hated May's flamboyant style. He was derided as the "Bill Veeck of the fairways." When he tried to make players easier to identify by having them wear numbers, the stuffier pros pinned those numbers to the seats of their pants. Yet May's innovations were not limited to flash. At a time when the PGA was still segregated, he invited African American pros to play in his events.

In 1953 the World's Championship became the first golf tournament to be nationally televised. Its conclusion was doubly memorable. Needing a birdie-three on the final hole to tie for the lead, Lew Worsham hit a 110-yard wedge to the green. The ball landed short, then rolled and rolled and finally fell into the cup for a winning eagle-two. "How about that?" announcer Jimmy Demaret shouted on-air. "The son-of-a-bitch went in!"

May's World Championship had by far the richest prize list in golf. The year after Worsham's heroics, he boosted first prize to $50,000, more than

Are you as good as Lew Worsham? The home hole at Tam Golf Course in Niles. *Photograph by the author.*

eight times the amount paid to the winner of the U.S. Open. Then, in 1958, May abruptly canceled his tournaments.

Different explanations have been given for May's action. Some sources say the pros wanted a bigger voice in running the events. Others claim that May felt the PGA was taking too big a slice of the gate receipts. Or maybe it was something else. Whatever the reason, it was over.

George S. May died in 1962. A few years later, his widow sold Tam O' Shanter to a developer, who converted most of the property into an industrial park. But bits of the old track remain in the nine-hole executive Tam Golf Course, operated by the Village of Niles. And on the home hole, golfers can still try their skill (and luck) at duplicating Lew Worsham's historic wedge shot.

# GOING STAGG

Amos Alonzo Stagg did not invent football. But during his forty-one years at the University of Chicago, he developed much of the modern game.

The son of a shoemaker, Stagg was born in New Jersey in 1862. He entered Yale University as a divinity student in 1884. While working odd jobs to pay his tuition, he became the star pitcher on the Yale baseball team. He began getting noticed, and six different major league teams tried to entice him away from school. The New York Nationals topped the bidding, with a contract for $4,200, quite a sum for a poor young scholar.

Stagg turned down all the offers. Professional baseball had an unsavory reputation, and he had personal reservations about playing sports for money. During his last year at Yale, he went out for the football team, and found his niche there. Playing end on the varsity squad, he was named to the very first All-American Team in 1889.

Stagg wanted to remain connected with football after graduation. For two years he coached at the YMCA College in Springfield, Massachusetts. This was at the same time that James Naismith was inventing basketball at the school, and some sources indicate that Stagg had a hand in the development of the new sport.

Then, in 1892, the brand-new University of Chicago hired Stagg to take charge of its athletic program. He was given a sizeable budget and faculty rank, something no full-time coach had ever had at any institution of higher learning. His title was director of the Division of Physical Culture.

University of Chicago professor Amos Alonzo Stagg, who also did a little coaching. *Author's collection.*

Though he never became a minister, Stagg felt he could promote the Christian ethic through football. "The coaching profession is one of the noblest and most far-reaching in building manhood," he once said. Of course, that didn't mean he had to field a losing team.

And Stagg's teams were winners. The University of Chicago Maroons won seven Big Ten Championships between 1899 and 1924. The undefeated 1905 and 1913 teams were ranked number-one in the nation.

Stagg was an innovator. He invented the huddle, the direct pass from center, the lateral, the man-in-motion, the backfield shift, and cross-blocking. Wanting his players to develop stamina along with strength, Stagg also introduced wind sprints. He was also the first to put numbers on uniforms. "All football comes from Stagg," Knute Rockne once declared.

But at the University of Chicago, football wasn't Stagg's only responsibility. He ran the entire athletic program. At different times, he coached baseball, basketball, track, and swimming. Oh, and while he was at it, he also invented the batting cage.

Outside of sports, Stagg led a sedate life. He didn't smoke or drink, went to church, raised a family, and stayed married to the same woman. At the same time, he wasn't shy about expressing his opinions. Stagg didn't like college fraternities. He also thought that professional football was a "menace" to amateur athletics.

In 1929 Robert Maynard Hutchins became the university's president. His vision didn't include high-powered football teams, and when Stagg turned seventy in 1932, Hutchins forced him to retire. But Stagg wasn't going to go quietly. He told the press he was leaving against his will.

Moving to California, Stagg signed on as the head coach at College of the Pacific. Again he built winning teams. In 1943, at the age of eighty-one, he was named the College Football Coach of the Year.

Stagg retired from the Pacific job in 1946. He had 314 wins to his credit—the most of any football coach. He then went to work for his son as an assistant coach at Susquehanna University. In 1951 the grand old man of football was elected a charter member of the College Football Hall of Fame as a player and as a coach. He was the only person honored in both categories.

Stagg celebrated his one hundredth birthday in 1962. When asked by a reporter about his future plans, Stagg quipped, "I may go on forever—statistics say that very few men die after the age of 100."

He almost made it to 103, dying in the spring of 1965. Today he is memorialized in a number of athletic fields in various cities, and Amos Alonzo Stagg High Schools in both Illinois and California.

# CHICAGO'S FORGOTTEN BASKETBALL TEAMS

The Chicago Bulls have been around since 1966. Before that, the city hosted a number of other professional basketball teams.

One of the earliest professional basketball leagues was the American Basketball League (ABL), which began playing in 1925. The Chicago franchise was awarded to Bears' owner George Halas, who naturally named his basketball team the Bruins. Like the National Football League of that era, the ABL operated on a shoestring. The Great Depression killed both the Bruins and the basketball league in 1931.

A new ABL was launched in 1933, but without a Chicago team. The rival National Basketball League (NBL) joined the fun four years later, also without a team in Chicago. Both leagues operated on that shoestring. Salaries were so low that the players all held full-time jobs doing something else. In 1939 the NBL added a new team with an old name, the Chicago Bruins.

Meanwhile, a team of African Americans was barnstorming around the country. Though they called themselves the Harlem Globetrotters to identify with the cultural capital of Black America, they were based in Chicago. The 'Trotters played serious, competitive ball in those days. In 1940 they won the World Professional Basketball Tournament, certifying them as the sport's best team.

The team the 'Trotters defeated in the tournament finals was none other than the Chicago Bruins. The Bruins remained in the NBL, with mediocre results, through the end of the 1941–42 season. The team was then replaced by the Chicago Studebaker Flyers. World War II was on, and some industrial companies sponsored professional basketball squads to garner publicity and boost morale. Among the other NBL teams of the era were the Toledo Jeeps, Akron Goodyear Wingfoots, and Fort Wayne Zollner Pistons.

The Studebaker Flyers lasted one season. After a year without a Chicago franchise, the NBL added the Chicago American Gears for the 1944–45 season. The team was sponsored by Maurice White and his American Gear & Manufacturing Company. The Gears played their first season home games at the Chicago Coliseum and missed the playoffs. For their second season, they moved to the much-smaller Cicero Stadium. Again they missed the playoffs.

By now the war had ended. For the 1946–47 season, a new professional basketball league was founded to challenge the NBL. The Basketball Association of America (BAA) had eleven teams, including the Chicago Stags. But the big news came when the Gears announced they'd signed DePaul star George Mikan. The six-foot-nine center was the hottest prospect in the sport. His five-year contract was for a hefty $60,000.

With Mikan in tow, the Gears moved to the International Amphitheater, finally made the playoffs, and went on to win the 1947 NBL championship. Then Maurice White got into a dispute with the other owners. He pulled the Gears out of the NBL and organized the Professional Basketball League of America. The league died after a month, and so did the Gears.

Over in the BAA, the 1946–47 Stags topped the Western Division but lost in the playoffs. Two mediocre seasons followed. In 1949 the BAA and the NBL merged to form the National Basketball Association (NBA). After one more mediocre season in the new NBA, the Stags folded.

Chicago was without professional basketball for a decade. In 1961 the NBA returned with an expansion team, the Chicago Packers. The Chicago Stock Yards was still operating, and since the team played at the Amphitheater, the name seemed appropriate. The Packers finished at the bottom of the league. One bright spot on the team was center Walt Bellamy, who was named NBA Rookie of the Year.

Predictably, the team's name had not gone down well. How many Chicagoans do you think were willing to say they were Packers fans? So, for the 1962–63 season, the team became the Zephyrs. However, this was the year Loyola University won the NCAA Basketball Championship, and that probably dampened interest in the humdrum professional team. When the season ended, the Zephyrs moved to Baltimore and became the Bullets.

Finally, we have the Chicago Majors of yet another American Basketball League. This ABL was launched in the fall of 1961. The Majors were owned by 'Trotters founder Abe Saperstein and played at the Chicago Stadium. The team and league went out of business midway through their second season. The ABL's main legacy is the three-point shot.

# 5.

# THE CHICAGO WAY

## WHERE HAVE YOU GONE, TERRIBLE TOMMY?

Tommy O'Connor was a young punk who specialized in armed robbery in the area around Maxwell Street. To the newspapers of 1920 Chicago, he was Lucky Tommy O'Connor. One witness to his crimes conveniently disappeared. A turncoat accomplice turned up conveniently dead. When O'Connor was brought to trial for the killing of a railroad cop, another accomplice fingered him in court as the killer—and still, he was acquitted.

Then, in the spring of 1921, O'Connor killed a Chicago policeman who was trying to arrest him. Lucky Tommy escaped, but a few weeks later, he was caught in Minneapolis. He was brought back to Chicago, put on trial for murder and, this time, was found guilty. He was sentenced to hang on December 15.

*Had Lucky Tommy finally run out of luck?* To anyone who would listen, he boasted that he'd never hang.

O'Connor was housed with the general inmate population in the fourth-floor cellblock of the Cook County Criminal Courts building on the Near North Side. Things were quiet there at 9:30 a.m. on Sunday, December 11. The cells were open, and prisoners were exercising in the common area of the cellblock. A single guard was on duty.

Suddenly, O'Connor produced a gun. He took the guard's keys, bound and gagged the man, and locked him in a cell. Then O'Connor opened the gate to the cellblock. With four companions, he walked out.

On the third floor, O'Connor's group subdued three more guards. Next they took a freight elevator to the basement, where they overpowered a fifth guard, as well as five trusties. The escapees then ran across the yard, climbed over a shed, and dropped down into the alley behind the jail.

By this time the alarm had been sounded. Two guards rushed out of the building just in time to see O'Connor jump on the running board of a passing car and force the driver, at gunpoint, to get him the hell out of there.

Lucky Tommy had done it again, and the city was in an uproar. To many, his escape seemed like an inside job. The *Tribune* noted that rumors of a planned break had been circulating for days prior to O'Connor's escape. States Attorney Robert Crowe wondered how O'Connor had gotten the gun and why only one guard was present. Chicago police chief Charles Fitzmorris flatly declared, "[O'Connor] was undoubtedly allowed to go by certain of the prison authorities."

Two of O'Connor's companions had immediately been recaptured. The other two were caught later. Tommy O'Connor was never seen again.

As time passed, O'Connor-sightings were reported in various places around the Midwest, and the legend grew. One story said O'Connor had gone to Ireland to fight for the IRA. Another claimed he had repented his wicked ways and become a Trappist monk. The small-time crook Lucky Tommy was transformed into Terrible Tommy, the scourge of the Windy City.

*Daily News* columnist Ben Hecht wrote a haunting piece that imagined O'Connor's everyday life and thoughts while in hiding. Hecht and his colleague Charles MacArthur also penned *The Front Page*, a play based partly on O'Connor's escape. Yet today, Terrible Tommy is not mentioned for his crimes, nor for his escape, nor even for the literature that sprang from that escape.

If you see this man, notify police! Fugitive Tommy O'Connor. *Author's collection.*

Tommy O'Connor had been sentenced to be "hanged by the neck until dead." A few years after his escape, when the state abandoned hanging in favor of the electric chair, someone decided that the gallows had to be saved in case O'Connor were ever recaptured. So, the gallows was taken apart and stored.

In 1929 the new Cook County Jail opened at Twenty-Sixth Street and California Avenue. The gallows was moved there. Now decades passed. In 1973 a man who had heard the O'Connor's story wrote to *Chicago Today* about the gallows. Columnist Kenan Heise investigated and found that the disassembled gallows was still lodged in the boiler room of the court building next to the jail.

A few more years went by. In 1977 officials concluded that they weren't likely to see O'Connor any time soon, so the macabre keepsake was finally sold to a museum.

Comments on this story should be addressed to the Institute for the Study of the Bureaucratic Mind.

# GROSS CYRANO

*Cyrano de Bergerac* is the most famous work of the French playwright Edmond Rostand. It tells of an adventurer who believes he is too ugly to win the heart of a lady, so instead, he helps his handsome friend court her. The tale has also been filmed many times, most notably with Jose Ferrer. What's less well known is that Rostand may have stolen the story from a Chicago businessman.

During the last years of the nineteenth century, Samuel Eberly Gross became a major land developer in and around Chicago. He claimed to have built more than ten thousand homes. Alta Vista Terrace in Wrigleyville was one of his smaller projects, but probably the most celebrated.

Gross had literary skills. He composed all of the advertising copy for his developments himself, and he tinkered with verse. In 1880 he wrote a play titled *The Merchant Prince of Cornville*. While on a visit to Paris that year, he submitted the manuscript to a number of actors and theatrical producers without success. Then he laid the play aside.

In 1895 Gross finally got around to publishing *The Merchant Prince*. The following year the play had a limited stage run in London. At that time Gross secured both British and American copyrights on his work.

Meanwhile, *Cyrano de Bergerac* debuted in Paris on December 28, 1897. Sometime later, Gross happened to read a review of Rostand's play and was struck by the similarities between *Cyrano* and *The Merchant Prince*. Then he received a letter from a New York friend pointing out the same thing. Gross decided to investigate the matter more fully.

He found several parallels between the two works. He also discovered that the actor in the title role of *Cyrano* was one of the actors who'd read *The*

An advertisement for S.E. Gross's play, at the time the court upheld his plagiarism suit. *From the* Chicago Tribune, *May 22, 1902.*

*Merchant Prince* manuscript back in 1880. That was too much of a coincidence for Gross. When *Cyrano* opened in Chicago early in 1899, he sued in federal court for plagiarism.

The lawsuit caused a sensation—*Cyrano* was one of the most popular plays of its day. "The whole thing is ridiculous," the Chicago producer told reporters. "Mr. Rostand is a gentleman, a scholar, and a poet." The claim that he had plagiarized another man's work was "simply absurd."

Gross was known as an aggressive marketer. Cynics suggested that the lawsuit was nothing more than a stunt to publicize his real estate business. Though the two plays were similar, Rostand's work clearly had greater literary merit. And as the *Chicago Times* noted, neither work was wholly original. "The handsome suitor as proxy for a deformed one is old at least as Boccaccio," the paper said.

The plagiarism suit wound its way through the courts for three years. Questions were raised about whether the French actor had shared the plot of Gross's play with Rostand. Similarities in the characters' names were noted. In full, thirty different parallels between *The Merchant Prince* and *Cyrano* were enumerated, including a balcony scene in which the main character stands in the shadows and whispers instructions to his friend.

"Gross Triumphs in Cyrano Suit" read the *Tribune* headline on May 22, 1902. Judge C.C. Kohlstaad had ruled that Rostand had indeed plagiarized Gross. United States theater companies were banned from staging *Cyrano*. Feeling vindicated, Gross settled instead for a nominal damage award of one dollar.

Rostand himself was not happy with being labeled a literary thief. He issued a sarcastic statement "admitting" to plagiarizing a number of other works, including "purloining from the house of a Louisiana ship owner a great piece on Joan of Arc."

Samuel Eberly Gross died in 1913. By that time, he was nearly broke, a victim of the vicissitudes of the real estate market. Over the course of a century, his name has been erased from a few places. The village of Grossdale, which he founded, is now Brookfield. Gross Avenue in Chicago is now McDowell Avenue. And while there is a Gross Park in the city, it's named for another man.

In 2008 the Brookfield school district tried to change the name of its S.E. Gross Middle School. Someone had discovered that Gross had been involved in a messy divorce when he was sixty-six years old. But students and parents protested, and the board dropped the matter.

# A Different Saint Valentine's Day Story

Most people who know some Chicago history know about the Saint Valentine's Day Massacre. On February 14, 1929, seven men were gunned down in the SMC Cartage Garage at 2122 North Clark Street. The dead men were involved in Bugs Moran's North Side bootlegging operation. The killings were likely ordered by rival gang lord Al Capone.

After ninety years, there's not much new to be said about the massacre itself. This story is about a neglected postscript.

The original *Scarface* was one of the great movie hits of 1932. As the name suggests, it's a thinly disguised biography of Capone. Paul Muni is the star. Onetime city beat reporter Ben Hecht wrote the screenplay, so the film carries the stamp of authenticity.

About halfway through the story, Muni decides to eliminate rival mobster Boris Karloff (yes, *that* Boris Karloff). Karloff learns about the plot and disappears. But he can't stay put. One night he goes bowling.

Meanwhile, Muni is at the opera when word comes that Karloff has been spotted. So, Muni and a few henchmen head for the bowling alley. And they don't take their bowling equipment with them.

Out on the lanes, Karloff is happily spilling pins. Muni and his friends enter unseen. "Just watch this one," Karloff tells the guy next to him. He grabs his ball and trots to the line.

Just as Karloff lets go of the ball, gunshots ring out, and he crumples to the floor. But the camera follows the ball down the lane. The ball hits the pins, and they scatter—all except the 10-pin, which spins crazily in circles a few times before finally falling over.

Film critics loved the bowling scene. They praised director Howard Hawks and his use of a slowly toppling pin as a symbol of Karloff dying offscreen. In fact, the whole idea of killing off a character in a bowling alley was brilliantly original. That had never been done.

Gangland applauded the film, too. Members of the Capone mob were tickled to see their exploits portrayed on the giant screen in glorious black-and-white. Among those members was one Vincent Gebardi, better known by his alias Machine Gun Jack McGurn.

As one of Capone's chief lieutenants, McGurn was credited as the lead gunman in that notorious Saint Valentine's Day Massacre. Yet he did not fit the public image of a gangster. He dressed conservatively in charcoal gray suits and charmed those he met with his gracious manners. He could discuss history and literature insightfully. Disdaining the wicked city where he made his livelihood, he owned a bungalow in sedate, suburban Oak Park.

McGurn was also a sportsman. As a golfer, he was good enough to qualify for the 1933 Western Open and play the first six holes under par—until some spoilsport cops turned up to arrest him. In the winter he was a bowler, carrying a 200-plus average. His favorite tenpin venue was Avenue Recreation on Milwaukee Avenue, just north of the Loop.

On Saint Valentine's evening in 1936, McGurn decided to go bowling. Along with two friends he drove into the city, arriving at Avenue Recreation around midnight. McGurn and his pals removed their outer clothing and prepared to bowl. Suddenly, three men burst in, waving pistols and announcing a stickup.

Most of the patrons dove for cover—as did McGurn's companions. Before McGurn could draw his own gun, one of the intruders ran up and pumped three slugs into him. Machine Gun Jack died on alley two with a house ball in his hands.

Within hours, the papers were on the street with extra editions. Since it had been Saint Valentine's Day, revenge was thought to be the motive for the killing. One homey touch was the unsigned valentine left on McGurn's body:

*You've lost your job,*
*You've lost your dough,*
*Your car and your fine houses.*
*But things could be worse, you know—*
*You haven't lost your trousers.*

The murder was never solved. Officially, it was credited to the usual "person or persons unknown." What's unmistakable is the eerie echo of Karloff's death in *Scarface*. Someone had seen the picture, been impressed by the staging, and decided to copy it. Once again, life imitates art.

# AN EDITOR'S SCOOP

In the days when Chicago had a dozen daily newspapers, competition was fierce. Beating the other papers to a good story was the big thing. If the facts sometimes suffered along the way, that was unimportant. As long as today's paper sold, nothing else mattered.

That's the theme of *The Front Page*—the play and its various movie incarnations. The tradition was already established in 1876, when the *Chicago Daily News* was founded.

The paper's first editor was Melville Stone. The son of a minister, Stone is remembered today as the distinguished general manager of the Associated Press. But he first learned his craft in the jungle of Chicago journalism.

Stone's *Daily News* was an afternoon paper. Among his competitors was the *Chicago Post & Mail*, which was published by two brothers named McMullen. Stone had worked for the McMullens before moving out on his own. He had no great fondness for them.

The *Post & Mail* and the rest of the afternoon papers were old-fashioned, dull and stodgy. Stone's paper was well-written and exciting. Soon the *Daily News* was selling more copies than any of its rivals. The McMullens fought back against the upstart in the simplest way possible. They began stealing stories from the *Daily News*.

*Chicago Daily News* editor Melville Stone. *Author's collection.*

The first edition of the *Daily News* came out at noon. Within three hours, the *Post & Mail* was on the street with much the same copy. Most of the time, the McMullens didn't bother to change a word. The pirating went on for weeks. Stone grew more and more frustrated—and more and more angry. He was particularly incensed when the brothers lifted a lively story on doings in the South Carolina legislature.

The climax of this conflict came on December 2, 1876. The noon edition of that day's *Daily News* trumpeted a disaster of epic proportions. There was a famine in Serbia.

Under the headline "Sad Story of Distress in Servia [*sic*]," the paper carried a report from an English traveler in the Balkans. He told of seeing a devastated land.

The people of Serbia were starving. Men, both young and old, were marching through the streets, crying out for food, cursing the rich for not doing more to help. Young women were wandering around in a state of semi-nudity. Children were dying by the thousands.

The country was descending into anarchy. The priests could no longer keep order. In one village, a group of women had led a riot in which a dozen houses had been pillaged and more than twenty people had been brutally murdered.

Conditions were especially bad in the provincial town of Slovik. With food running out and the population desperate, the mayor of Slovik had simply given up. He had said as much in an official proclamation, which ended with the ominous words: "Er us siht la Etsll iws nel lum cmeht." The paper translated the original Serbian as "the municipality cannot aid [anyone]."

So went the *Daily News* report of the famine in Serbia. It was a colorful, vivid account. And sure enough, the *Post & Mail* reprinted the same story in its entirety in its 3:00 p.m. edition. The headline was changed to "Horrid Starvation in Servia." But other than that, the text was identical to the original *Daily News* story. The *Post & Mail* copied everything, including the Serbian quotation.

That was what Melville Stone was waiting for. He had a surprise in store for the McMullen brothers.

December 2, 1876 was a Saturday. The *Daily News* did not publish on Sunday. But instead of waiting for Monday to spring his surprise, Stone contacted two morning papers, the *Tribune* and the *Times*. They were more than willing to help him in their own Sunday editions.

Now Stone revealed that the *Daily News* story of the Serbian famine had been a hoax. There was no English traveler, no riots, no dying children, no semi-nude women. The Serbian language proclamation from the mayor of Slovik was bogus. Read backward, it said: "The McMullens will steal this sure."

The McMullen brothers became the laughingstock of the city. Within months, the *Post & Mail* folded. Melville Stone's *Chicago Daily News* eventually folded, too, but not for another one hundred years.


# THE SHORT, UNHAPPY LIFE OF ALGREN STREET

In 1968 Chicago changed the name of South Park Way and South Park Avenue to Dr. Martin Luther King Jr. Drive. Renaming a street is expensive, both for the city and the people located on the street. But the tragic circumstances of King's murder overruled any concerns about cost. The change quickly went through.

Such a swift and smooth transition from one street name to another has not always been possible. Chicagoans are protective of their street names.

Nelsen Algren's apartment on Evergreen Avenue. *Photograph by the author.*

In 1924 the city council changed Western Avenue to Woodrow Wilson Road. Street signs went up, and the *Tribune* conducted interviews at the corner of "Woodrow Wilson Road and Washington Boulevard," asking passersby what they thought of the new name. Most responses were positive. But property owners complained, and within a month, the street was again Western Avenue.

In 1927 the council again tried to change a street name. Robey Street had been named for land developer James Robey, most likely by Robey himself. In June an ordinance was passed changing the street's name to Damen Avenue, after West Side pastor Father Arnold Damen. Again the property owners protested. This time the council didn't budge. Robey Street was gone for good, and Damen Avenue remained.

In 1933 Mayor Edward J. Kelly responded to pressure from the Polish voting bloc by having Crawford Avenue changed to Pulaski Road. This resulted in pressure from various groups that wanted the old name back. The Illinois Supreme Court finally ruled in favor of Pulaski Road after nineteen years of litigation.

All of these name changes involved major arterial streets. Renaming a little local street should not have been controversial. At least, that's what *Tribune* columnist Mike Royko thought when the great Chicago writer Nelson Algren died in 1981.

Algren had lived in a three-story walkup at 1958 West Evergreen Avenue for many years. He'd been one of Royko's friends. "It would be a nice gesture for [the city] to rename one of the little streets around Wicker Park after him," Royko wrote. "Algren Court or Algren Place. Nothing big. He wouldn't expect it."

That was in May. Early the next year, Royko received word that Mayor Jane Byrne had taken up his suggestion. Three blocks of Evergreen Avenue, between Milwaukee and Damen, would be renamed Algren Street. The mayor even sent Royko one of the new street signs.

The trouble started when city crews began putting up those signs. Algren had never been popular with the city's Polish community, as they thought his writings slandered them. There were still a lot of Poles living in Wicker Park in 1982. They didn't like the new street name.

Neither did some of the people who lived on Evergreen. Handbills began circulating around the neighborhood. They warned of all the problems and expenses a name change would cause. Residents would have to spend a small fortune revising their drivers' licenses and other official documents. Delivery men and visitors would get lost. Someone might even die if an ambulance couldn't locate an address.

Pressure was put on the aldermen to change the name back. In the meantime, activists began hanging cardboard signs that read, "Evergreen" over the Algren Street signs.

After a few weeks of this guerrilla warfare, the city gave in. It turned out that the crews had put up the Algren Street signs before the city council had officially voted on the mayor's proposal. The local alderman asked his colleagues to reject the name change, and they did. Evergreen Avenue remained Evergreen.

The whole business made an impression on the politicians. Shortly after the Algren Street debacle, Chicago began issuing honorary street names— those brown-and-white signs you see hung under the real street signs at hundreds of places around town. This way, some worthy person could be memorialized without arousing the voters' wrath.

I'd heard that the city had settled on making a few blocks of Evergreen Avenue an honorary Algren Street. But the last time I visited there, I didn't see one brown sign. And in front of Algren's old home, the Chicago Tribute Marker was tilting badly to one side. It looked as though it had been hit by a truck.

Some people have long memories.

# THE BOWLING BALL THAT WENT AROUND THE WORLD

In 1914 the Brunswick-Balke-Collender Company of Chicago was the world's largest manufacturer of bowling equipment. Until then, most bowlers had used wooden bowling balls. Now Brunswick came out with a hard rubber ball called the Mineralite. The company guaranteed that the vermillion-colored ball would not chip or lose its shape for three years.

Still, the twenty-dollar Mineralite price tag was pretty steep for 1914, about three times what bowlers paid for a wooden ball. Something had to be done to convince them to part with that much cash. Then a Brunswick manager came up with a grand idea—why not send the Mineralite around the world?

Travel was hard a century ago. Most people spent their entire lives within fifty miles of the place they were born. Yet the logistics were not as difficult as they might seem. The British Empire spanned the globe, and there were YMCAs in most of Britain's colonies. Brunswick would simply ship the ball from one YMCA to another. Regular reports would be sent back to Chicago, and bowlers could track the ball as it made its journey.

Brunswick Mineralite #391914 left the company's headquarters on Wabash Avenue on May 28, 1914. Two days later, it arrived in San Francisco. After a ceremony at the local YMCA, the ball was sent back across the country to New York. After another ceremony, the traveling Mineralite was put on a ship and delivered to London, where yet another ceremony was held. The ball's next scheduled stop was the International Bowling Tournament in Berlin.

At this point, things got complicated. While the ball was making its way to Berlin, war broke out between Germany and Britain—a little scrap that became known as World War I. The Mineralite arrived in Berlin, and German officials were suspicious. None of them had ever seen a big, American-style bowling ball. They thought it might be a bomb. So, the Germans sent the ball back. Somehow it wound up in Paris. After sitting around there for a few months, the French returned it to London.

Brunswick Mineralite bowling ball #391914 leaving San Francisco on its world tour. *Courtesy of the* Bowlers Journal.

The original plan had been to send the ball from Berlin to Vienna, then to Rome for a hoped-for blessing from the Pope. From Rome, it was to go to India. But because of the war, that wasn't going to work. The British finally decided to book passage for the ball on a merchant ship and send it directly through to India. It arrived in Bombay in November.

Once again, there was a ceremony at the YMCA. The Mineralite was then loaded onto a ship headed for Australia. A few days later, Brunswick received a terrible cable message—the ship carrying the ball had sunk in the Indian Ocean.

The Wabash Avenue office was plunged into gloom. But then, a second cable brought exciting news. The first report was wrong. The ball had missed the doomed ship and was still safe in Bombay!

Now the Mineralite really was put on board a ship and made its way to Australia without incident. From Sydney the ball sailed across the Pacific to San Diego, where it was exhibited at the California Pacific Exposition. Finally, on June 28, 1915, after thirteen months and thirty-five thousand miles on the road and over the sea, Mineralite #391914 arrived back in San Francisco. There it was proudly displayed in the Brunswick booth at the Panama Pacific World's Fair.

Then the fair closed, and Brunswick lost the ball. It was missing for nineteen years. But in 1934, a janitor found Mineralite #391914 tucked away in a plain cardboard box on a shelf in the back of the company warehouse.

In Chicago, there was another world's fair that year, the Century of Progress Exposition. Brunswick trotted out the lost-and-found Mineralite and again put it on display. Stories in the newspapers told of the amazing adventures of the world-traveling bowling ball. The public came, they saw, and they were impressed.

Then the Chicago fair closed. And once again, the ball disappeared.

*What happened to it?* Nobody knows. But if you come across an old vermillion-colored bowling ball with serial #391914 at a flea market, buy it. You'll then own a piece of history.

# BERTILLONAGE IN CHICAGO

For a dozen years around the turn of the twentieth century, Chicago was hailed as the world leader in the never-ending fight against crime. Science had shown the way. The city had adopted and fully implemented Bertillonage.

If you were arrested in Chicago in the year 1900, you learned that Bertillonage involved a system of booking procedures. At the police station you were photographed both full-face and profile. The officer in charge then made a note of your eye color. Then began the measurements—the heart of the system.

First you stood against a calibrated wall so that your height could be determined. Next you were told to sit down, and the officer measured the distance from the bench seat to the top of your head. Then out came the calipers to check the length and width of your head. Next you stood up again and stretched out your arms sideways so the officer could measure the distance from left middle fingertips to right middle fingertips. Then the officer measured the lengths of your left middle fingers, left little fingers, left feet, left forearms, and right ears. Finally, the officer measured the distance from your left nostril to the bottom of your left ear. That made eleven measurements in all.

In essence, Bertillonage was an exercise in the laws of probability. Many people might have one measured factor in common, such as height. Fewer people would have two factors in common. Even fewer people would have three factors in common. And so on. *How many people would have all eleven factors in common—all eleven measurements identical?* The odds of that happening were calculated as approximately 260 million to 1. With those odds, the system was considered a foolproof method of identification.

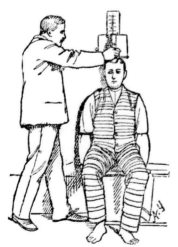

MEASUREMENT OF THE TRUNK.

One of the measurements used in Bertillonage. *From the* Chicago Tribune, *February 26, 1888.*

Bertillonage was named for its inventor, Alphonse Bertillon. In 1880 he was a young, low-level clerk in the Paris Police Department. Working in his spare time, he developed his system of precise physical measurements. He finally convinced his skeptical superiors to adopt his idea after he successfully identified a number of repeat offenders. Before the decade was over, Bertillonage was used in all French prisons and was being tried in Russia, Japan, and other countries.

The system was introduced to the United States in 1887 by Warden Robert W. McClaughry at the Illinois State Prison in Joliet. This caught the attention of the *Chicago Tribune*, which ran a lengthy article on Bertillonage on February 26, 1888. Three years later, McClaughry was appointed superintendent of the Chicago Police Department. He immediately began implementing Bertillonage on a citywide basis.

Chicago was to host the Columbian Exposition World's Fair in 1893. Along with the hundreds of thousands of respectable visitors, there were to be a certain number of crooks coming to town. McClaughry intended to be ready for the disreputables.

The city council had already increased the size of the police force. Now McClaughry began collecting Bertillon measurements from foreign countries, prisons, and other sources. By the time the fair opened he had thousands of prospective criminals in his files. The superintendent assured the public that those who were planning to prey on the community would be given "enforced seclusion" during the fair.

Chicago continued to expand Bertillonage after the fair closed. McClaughry sent his son to Paris to study with the master firsthand. The emperor of Austria requested details on how Chicago used the system. Every so often, the local papers would run a story about a crook who was tripped up by his Bertillon file. By 1903 the city had over fifty thousand people registered in its rogues collection.

Yet flaws in the system were becoming apparent. For one thing, body measurement would work only if the subject had reached physical maturity, which meant that Bertillonage was not effective in dealing with juveniles. Then two cases of different individuals having the same exact measurements were splashed across the press. Even Robert McClaughry, who had become warden of the federal prison at Leavenworth, became convinced that fingerprinting was the better method of identification,

Chicago was gradually weaned off Bertillonage. Finally, after sitting unused for over twenty years, the city's sixty-five thousand Bertillon records were cleared out of police headquarters and sent off to a warehouse in 1960. Presumably they are still there.

# WAITERS' REVENGE?

In 1903 Chicago saloonkeeper Mickey Finn became notorious for drugging patrons' drinks so he could rob them. Though Mickey was long gone by 1918, he was once again front-page news on the morning of June 22 that year. During a raid on union headquarters, 150 local waiters were taken into custody. They were suspected of serving Mickey Finn cocktails.

The raid was conducted by State's Attorney Maclay Hoyne. During the previous two weeks, nearly two dozen people, including Mayor Thompson, had become violently ill after dining in downtown restaurants. The Hotel Sherman had hired a detective agency to investigate. The detectives found that the victims had been given drinks laced with an emetic powder. Further digging traced the powder to the union headquarters.

The substance came in envelopes labeled "Mickey Finn Powder—12 doses triple strength." Printed directions on the envelope innocuously described the contents as "the great liquor antidote for drunkenness." It could be dissolved in beer, tea, coffee, soup, or any other liquid. No more than one dose was to be administered every twenty-four hours to adults only.

The world was in turmoil in June 1918. While the Great War dragged on, the Bolsheviks had seized power in Russia and were promoting other revolutions. Chicagoans remembered the anarchist poison outrage at Archbishop Mundelein's installation banquet a few years earlier. So, those 150 waiters had been rounded up.

Though most of the waiters were quickly set free, six men were arrested on charges of conspiracy and assault to do bodily harm. They included waiters' union president Ben Parker, two other union officers, and three waiters. The six men were then released on bond.

One of the three waiters arrested was W. Stuart Wood. He had gotten the Mickey Finn powder from a St. Louis drug company and was selling it at union headquarters for twenty cents a packet. According to the state's attorney, the waiters had been using the Mickey Finn powder to punish patrons who were stingy with tips.

Union president Parker vigorously denied the accusations. Speaking at a joint meeting of allied unions, Parker claimed that State's Attorney Hoyne was engaged in political showboating. The raids were a stunt. Union officials would gladly have met with Hoyne, if only he had asked them. According to Parker, the Mickey Finn story had been dreamed up by the hotel and restaurant owners to discredit the union.

The hotel and restaurant owners had a different slant. This was more than a simple case of individual waiters using Mickey Finn powder to "discipline" tightwad patrons. They speculated this was actually a union plot to intimidate businesses that wouldn't meet union demands. There was talk that the notorious labor racketeer Moss Enright was behind the scheme.

In July the grand jury heard testimony from forty-nine witnesses in the Mickey Finn cocktail case. Indictments were returned against ten men—

Can you trust your waiter? *From the* Caney Daily Chronicle, *July 16, 1920.*

Parker, Wood, the other four who had been arrested in June, and four additional waiters. The ten were charged with conspiracy to do bodily harm and injure the public health.

"Waiters Drugged Hotel Patrons"—that was the sort of headline that caught a reader's eye. Over the next several months, the story of Chicago's Mickey Finn cocktails was reprinted in dozens of newspapers throughout the country. Often the story was accompanied by a cartoon of a tuxedoed waiter surreptitiously pouring the contents of an envelope into a mixing bowl. Copycat waiters were allegedly using the Mickey Finn powders in New York, Cleveland, Portland, and other cities. As late as 1920, one Kansas paper was reprinting the story as if it were breaking news.

Meanwhile, back in Chicago, nothing happened. The charges against the ten indicted conspirators seemed to have been dropped. State's Attorney Maclay Hoyne did run for mayor of Chicago as a reform candidate in 1919, but finished third. The next year he lost a bid for a third term in the Democratic primary.

Ben Parker was voted out as president of the waiters' union in 1920. He was later unsuccessful in claiming Native American ancestry for a share of oil land in Oklahoma. When he died in 1943, his obituary identified him as "President of the Chicago Waiters' Alliance."

# SIC TRANSIT GLORIA HINKY DINK

Michael Kenna was known as Hinky Dink because he was a little man. Yet during the first half of the twentieth century, he cast a giant shadow in Chicago politics—if not actually in power, then certainly in image.

Kenna was the model of the saloonkeeper politician. His bailiwick was the First Ward, which included the Loop and stretched down to Twenty-Second Street (Cermak Road) and the vice district known as the Levee. Besides serving inexpensive beverages and free lunch, Kenna's establishments also provide cheap lodging for down-and-outers who could be counted on to vote as he directed. The most famous of his places was the Workingmen's Exchange at 426 South Clark Street.

In 1897 Kenna joined Bathhouse John Coughlin in the city council as one of the First Ward's two aldermen. The two men complemented each other—Coughlin was big and loud, while Kenna preferred to work behind the scenes. For the next four decades, they conducted a virtual master class on Urban Politics for Fun and Profit.

After Coughlin died in 1938, Kenna continued on alone. Past eighty now, he seldom emerged from his hotel suite. His mind wandered, though some days he was as sharp as ever. Coughlin blew through cash as fast as he collected it—and often faster. Kenna held onto his money. He was reckoned to be a millionaire several times over when he died on October 9, 1946.

Kenna had once been married to Catherine Devro, a devout Irishwoman who shunned the spotlight. While her husband ran his saloon, she had become a temperance worker. Mrs. Kenna had died several years earlier. The marriage had been childless, so Hinky Dink's estate became a matter of contention.

"Rush to Claim Hinky Dink's Millions Is On," read the headline in the *Tribune* a week after Kenna's death. Bank officials had estimated the late alderman's fortune ran as high as $9 million. Already, dozens of prospective heirs were coming out of the woodwork and lawyering up.

The list was long and confusing. John Kenna, Hinky Dink's father, had been married twice, producing a total of six children. This fact was disputed

Hinky Dink Kenna's eighty-five-dollar grave marker in Calvary Cemetery. *Photograph by the author.*

by a man who claimed to be the descendant of a third John Kenna marriage. Thus, Hinky Dink had three full siblings, and at least two—or maybe more— half-siblings. And unlike the alderman, these Kennas had been fruitful and multiplied. Meanwhile, relatives of Hinky Dink's late wife were also after a share of the wealth.

When Hinky Dink's six safe deposit boxes were finally opened, the contents were disappointing, with a mere $872,000 in cash and securities on hand. The size of the estate was revised downward to a paltry $1.3 million. The alderman's will, dated 1935, detailed bequests to more than seventy individuals, including relatives, politicians, and friends. The largest single bequest was $30,000 for the construction of his mausoleum.

Months passed. Now it was 1947. A woman came forward saying she was Hinky Dink's lovechild. Another woman claimed to be a long-lost half-sister. An auction of the alderman's personal effects brought in $5,129. In August Kenna's gross estate was officially pegged at $1,014,000. After deducting $368,000 for taxes and various legal fees, $646,000 remained. The seventy-two detailed bequests took $209,000. That left $437,000 to be split among seventeen heirs.

Two more years went by. The final accounting of the Kenna estate took place in July 1949. An additional $66,000 was distributed to the heirs. Of that amount, $36,000 came from an unneeded tax reserve. The remaining $30,000 was the money that had been set aside for the alderman's mausoleum.

Years before, Hinky Dink's wife, Catherine, had been buried in a simple grave at Calvary Cemetery. The alderman had planned to have her rest next to him in his mausoleum. But Catherine Devro Kenna's relatives were miffed at being shut out of her husband's estate. They refused permission for her to be moved, so the mausoleum was never built.

Still, Hinky Dink's heirs did not forget him. After splitting the $30,000 mausoleum fund, they purchased an eighty-five-dollar slab to mark his final resting place. If you root around in the grass at Calvary Cemetery, you might be able to find it.

# 6.
# FORGOTTEN CHICAGO
# MOVIES

## *IN OLD CHICAGO* (1937)

Most films about historic Chicago seem to be about Prohibition-era gangsters. But in 1937, when *In Old Chicago* was released, Prohibition had just ended, and gangster movies had the flavor of current events documentaries. *In Old Chicago* reached further back into the city's history, to the Great Fire of 1871. It has its own share of shady characters, too.

Twentieth Century-Fox spent $1.8 million making the movie, a hefty price tag in 1937. Much of the budget went into the climactic fire scenes. Of course, the whole epic was filmed on a Hollywood soundstage, so *In Old Chicago*'s special effects look primitive to modern eyes. Still, the studio did undertake extensive research, basing the sets on old pictures from the actual fire.

From a historian's standpoint, the problem with the film is the story. The screenplay is nearly all fiction. About the only true facts are that a fire starts in the O'Leary barn, and Chicago burns down.

The movie opens in 1854 in the dune lands of Indiana, with the Irish O'Leary family in a horse-drawn wagon on their way to the up-and-coming city of Chicago. And right away, tragedy strikes.

Dad O'Leary tries to race a railroad train and is killed in an accident before he makes it to the Promised Land. After Dad is buried in the dunes, his widow, Molly (Alice Brady), is left to soldier on alone with her three young sons. Molly finally gets to Chicago, and like a good Irishwoman, she starts a laundry—in 1937, filmmakers didn't worry about perpetuating ethnic stereotypes.

Chicago grows. The O'Leary boys grow. Handsome, roguish Dion (Tyrone Power) becomes a gambler. Boring-but-honest Jack (Don Ameche) sets himself up as a lawyer. The third brother hangs around the other two.

Alice Faye plays the female lead, a saloon singer who is courted by the two main O'Leary brothers. Brian Donlevy is her boss and a political wheeler-dealer, the movie's villain. Sidney Blackmer, who made a career portraying Teddy Roosevelt, is cast here as a different historic figure, General Philip Sheridan. Andy Devine provides comic relief, and Rondo Hatton lurks about looking sinister.

At length, Jack is elected mayor of Chicago. He's a reformer and has vowed to clean up the city's gambling dens. This brings him into conflict with Dion. But before the brothers can have a showdown, the family cow kicks over a lantern in the O'Leary barn, and things start burning.

The movie climaxes with twenty minutes of the Great Fire. All the tangled plot points are settled. And incidentally, the city is destroyed.

In 1937, disaster movies were the latest fashion in Hollywood. *San Francisco* had been a blockbuster hit for MGM in 1936. So, when Twentieth Century-

*In Old Chicago*—has anyone seen the O'Leary boys? *From* Harper's Weekly, *October 28, 1871.*

Fox decided to make its own disaster epic, that studio kept much of the plot from the MGM story and simply replaced the earthquake with a fire.

Some of the parallels between the two films are unintentionally hilarious. In the earthquake scenes of *San Francisco*, Clark Gable wanders around in a daze with a bloodstain down his right cheek. In the climax of *In Old Chicago*, Tyrone Power wanders around with a similar bloodstain—but it's on his *left* cheek.

And the shameless copying actually succeeded. *In Old Chicago* was praised by the critics and became one of the top-grossing films of 1937. The movie was nominated for six Academy Awards, including Best Picture, and wound up winning two. Second-unit director Robert D. Webb, who was in charge of the fire scenes, took home the Oscar for Best Assistant Director. Alice Brady and her Irish accent won for Best Supporting Actress.

(At the Academy Awards Ceremony, a man stepped forward to accept the award for Brady, who was at home sick. It turned out that Brady had not sent him. That particular Oscar statue was never seen again.)

As I've said, the movie is full of historical inaccuracy. I'll mention just one—the real-life Mrs. O'Leary was named Catherine, not Molly. But if you don't mind watching old black-and-white films and can overlook some plot holes, *In Old Chicago* is 114 fast-moving minutes of vintage entertainment.

## CITY THAT NEVER SLEEPS (1953)

Liza Minnelli sang that she wanted to "wake up in a city that never sleeps." Frank Sinatra sang the same thing. They were singing about New York, but they had the wrong place. The city that never sleeps is Chicago.

In 1953 Republic Pictures released a movie set in Chicago with that title— *City That Never Sleeps*. Republic specialized in low-budget serials, Westerns, and action-adventure stories. *City That Never Sleeps* was the studio's version of film noir—a crime drama about desperate, imperfect people, shot in black-and-white, mostly at night. No one is neutral about film noir. You either love it or you hate it.

The movie opens with a tracking shot of the downtown Chicago skyline at dusk. Then comes an echoing voice, seemingly from heaven: "I am the city. Hub and heart of America. Melting pot of every race, creed, color, and religion in humanity." And so on.

This is the Voice of Chicago, courtesy of veteran character actor Chill Wills. So, even before we get to a plot, we have a major mystery—why did the studio cast someone with such an unmistakable Texas accent?

Now we are introduced to the characters in the drama. Johnny Kelly (Gig Young) is an unhappy cop who wants to quit the force and dump his wife. He talks about running off to California with Angel Face (Mala Powers). She came to Chicago intending to be a ballerina and wound up a stripper.

That's the recurring theme among the principal characters—everybody wanted to be something else. A performance artist known as the Mechanical Man (Wally Cassell) wanted to be an actor. A thug (William Talman) wanted to be a magician. The thug's lady love (Marie Windsor) has achieved her ambition of becoming a trophy wife but is tired of the job.

There is also Biddel (Edward Arnold), a corrupt lawyer. He's the only one who seems satisfied with his career path. But if the character Biddel is satisfied, I suspect that the real-life actor Edward Arnold was not. He was probably wishing he was back in Frank Capra's movies, where he got to play big-time corrupt characters.

(Speaking of actors, watch for Tom Poston as a plain-clothes cop. This was one of his first movie roles.)

*City That Never Sleeps* takes place during a single night in Chicago, the last night on duty for Officer Kelly before he resigns. But Kelly's partner is sick and has been replaced by a cop known as Sergeant Joe. And once Sergeant Joe opens his mouth, you realize it's our Voice of Chicago, Texas Chill Wills. Now the movie does seem like Capra, namely *It's a Wonderful Life.*

The night moves on. The police radio crackles with the crimes of the city. "Man beating a woman at 103$^{rd}$ and Avenue J…supermarket burglary on Addison Street…disturbance at Elston and Montrose…mugging on Hyde Park Boulevard." Things are really popping out there in the neighborhoods. But if you examine the scenery closely, you'll notice that most of the movie wasn't shot on location. It's actually a soundstage, a back lot, or the streets of Los Angeles.

The movie's running time is ninety minutes. The first hour is pretty slow. As the plot gradually unfolds, the major characters are thrown together.

The action picks up in the final twenty minutes. This part was clearly filmed in Chicago. (Hey, there's the Wrigley Building, all lit up!) The grand climax is a foot chase in the dark along the North Side "L" tracks.

With that, all the plot conflicts are resolved. The sun rises over the city. The Voice of Chicago returns to dispense final wisdom.

Like most Republic features, *City That Never Sleeps* did only moderate business. It was never considered a classic and can be best described as a good bad movie. However, in recent years, the film has been rediscovered by cinema buffs and has developed a cult following. Martin Scorsese is said to be among its biggest fans.

You can make your own call. Just don't complain to me about the Voice of Chicago.

# *AL CAPONE* (1959)

Al Capone was a celebrity in his time. Even when he was alive, they were making movies about him. *Little Caesar* came out in 1931, followed by the original *Scarface* a year later. Of course, since Capone was still around, the name of the lead character was changed. Much of the storyline was fiction, too. The filmmakers didn't want to be sued—or suffer more direct retaliation.

By 1959 Big Al was dead. Allied Artists, a second-tier Hollywood studio, felt it was finally safe enough to tell it like it was. The result was a film simply titled *Al Capone.*

The movie opens without credits. The camera pans slowly through a crowded, smoky saloon. The offscreen narrator introduces us to the "incredible era," just after the First World War. "It began in 1919," we are told. "The story of the bitter, ten-year fight that was waged between the rich and booming city of Chicago and a ruthless, cunning criminal."

Suddenly, the words "AL CAPONE" flash over the scene. The soundtrack explodes with a disjointed, jazzy tune. And then comes Rod Steiger, wandering in as a young, seedy-looking Capone. He's just arrived from Brooklyn. Johnny Torrio (Nehemiah Persoff) has brought him to town to work as a bodyguard and all-purpose thug.

Within a short time, Capone is arrested for beating up a speakeasy patron. That's when we meet our narrator, an honest cop named Schaefer (James Gregory). He wants to send Capone back to Brooklyn. But somebody downtown has made a phone call to Schaefer's boss, and Capone is released.

So, Schaefer goes back to narrating. Prohibition is coming, and there is big money to be made in bootlegging. Then we move into the saga of Capone's rise to the top. We see all the familiar events of Chicago gangland in the 1920s. Most of them are presented accurately.

Any movie called *Al Capone* is going to be a "guy" movie. The studio probably figured the wives and girlfriends who were dragged along to see it might get bored, so they introduced a romantic interest named Maureen (Fay Spain). She's the widow of an innocent bystander who gets killed during one of Capone's operations.

Al is attracted to Maureen. She finds herself attracted to Al's sensitive side. The two become a couple. The movie suggests Maureen is Al's one true love. Nothing is said about the real Capone's wife and son.

Back in the action, we witness the Saint Valentine's Day Massacre and more history. By now, Honest Schaefer has moved up in the police department. He's the leader of a task force out to nail Capone. In the end, Schaefer gets his man. The movie concludes with Big Al in Alcatraz.

Rod Steiger chews into his role with great gusto. He shouts a lot, but can also quote Shakespeare and sing a bit of *Rigoletto*. Like most actors who've tackled the role, he is a few years too old to play Capone—who was just out of his teens when he went to work for Johnny Torrio.

It's interesting to watch Nehemiah Persoff as Torrio. His acting is very low-key. That same year, 1959, Persoff played another gang chief, Little Bonaparte, in *Some Like It Hot*. His performance in that film was way over the top. But of course, that film was a comedy.

*Al Capone* received good reviews and was a moderate success at the box office. And although it is by no means my favorite movie, it did change my life.

I was twelve when the movie premiered. One thing puzzled me. In the story, Capone and his crew are exiled to Cicero when Chicago elects a reform mayor named Dever. So, if Capone was so bad, why did Chicago later vote Dever out and bring back Big Bill Thompson?

My grandfather was a precinct captain and knew politics, so I asked him about it. "Dever was honest," Grandpa told me. "He just wasn't a very good politician." As if, in Chicago, the two qualities are mutually exclusive.

After that, I began reading anything I could find on William E. Dever. I eventually wrote my doctoral dissertation about him. It was later published as a book titled *The Mayor Who Cleaned Up Chicago*.

Thank you, Allied Artists!

# *GAILY, GAILY* (1969)

*The Front Page*, the 1928 play about Chicago newspaper reporters, has been made into a movie several times. The most-celebrated version is *His Girl Friday* (1940). The original work was written by two Chicago reporters, Charles MacArthur and Ben Hecht.

During the early 1960s, Hecht wrote a series of fictionalized memoirs about his days as a young Chicago reporter titled *Gaily, Gaily*. Those stories are the basis for a 1969 feature film of the same name. Though not as famous or as well-done as the various adaptations of *The Front Page*, the movie *Gaily, Gaily* is worth a watch.

The film was directed by Norman Jewison. In 1969 he had just finished *The Thomas Crown Affair*, a caper story, before taking on the Hecht project. Before that, Jewison had scored consecutive Oscar nominations for two decidedly different types of movies. *The Russians Are Coming! The Russians Are Coming!* was a 1966 comedy. *In the Heat of the Night* was a 1967 murder mystery with an underlying racial theme. To say that Jewison was a versatile director is an understatement.

*Gaily, Gaily*—young Ben Harvey, or Ben Hecht. *From the* New York Herald, *September 25, 1921.*

Beau Bridges stars in *Gaily, Gaily*. He'd been acting since he was a child, often working with his father Lloyd. Now in his mid-twenties, the younger Bridges was taking on a lead role for the first time.

*Gaily, Gaily* opens with a Hecht quotation—"If you did not believe in God, in the importance of marriage, in the United States government, in the sanity of politicians, in the wisdom of your elders, then you had to believe… in art." The statement tries to set the tone for the movie, telling viewers that what they'll be seeing is irreverent, witty, and profound. Actually, much of the film is played for slapstick.

In the film, the year is 1910. It is the Fourth of July in small-town Illinois. Here we meet Hecht's alter-ego, nineteen-year-old Ben Harvey (Bridges). He has come down with a mysterious malady that the local doctor can't identify. Ben's grandmother offers the simple, earthy answer—"His juices are all damned up!"

So, Ben sets off for Chicago. The proverbial rube from the sticks, he's soon relieved of his money. Ben is on the point of starving when rescue comes in the person of Queen Lil (Melina Mercouri). She gives Ben food and shelter in what he believes is her boardinghouse. He doesn't realize Lil's place is the biggest brothel in Chicago.

Francis Xavier Sullivan (Brian Keith) works at the *Chicago Journal* and is a friend of Queen Lil. Sullivan gets her innocent protégé hired as a reporter. Ben has various adventures in yellow journalism and has his eyes opened. Typical is the wisdom dispensed by one of the editors. "What does a sex maniac do?" he asks the rookie scribe before supplying the answer: "A good sex maniac sells newspapers!"

Meanwhile, Ben begins a tentative romance with one of Lil's young ladies, Adeline (Margot Kidder, in her breakout role). As this is Chicago, there's also a power struggle between two crooked politicians—the hypocrite reformer (George Kennedy) versus the unapologetic crook (Hume Cronyn). Ben winds up in the middle of it. Pursued in a frantic chase, he falls into the river, and…

*Gaily, Gaily* was budgeted at $8 million. That was a sizeable sum in 1969, and it shows. The movie is a visual treat. The production earned three Oscar nominations—Costume, Sound, and Art Direction/Set Direction—though it would be shut out in all three categories.

United Artists released the movie in December, hoping for a holiday season blockbuster. The reviews were mixed, and its box office performance was disappointing. Jewison, Bridges, and the rest went on with their lives and tried to forget *Gaily, Gaily*.

One small scene sums up the movie. A young man is reciting his new poem to some friends. "Hog Butcher for the World," he begins. "Tool Maker, Stacker of Wheat, Player with Railroads." And after a few lines, he stops, saying he hasn't finished it yet.

Of course, the young man is Carl Sandburg. The scene doesn't have anything to do with the plot, but for a few minutes, it's entertaining. And that's the best way to watch *Gaily, Gaily*. Don't think about whether it makes sense. Just enjoy the ride.

# *COOLEY HIGH* (1975)

*Cooley High* is comedy/drama centered on a group of African American teenagers in the mid-1960s. The movie was filmed in Chicago and released late in 1975. Because of some similarities, it is often referred to as "the Black *American Graffiti*."

Once there really was a Cooley High in Chicago. Named for one-time school superintendent Edward G. Cooley, it was located at 1225 North Sedgwick Street. The 1908 building had been the original Lane Tech and later housed the Washburne Trade School. In 1958 it was converted to Cooley Vocational High School and Upper Grade Center.

The screenplay for *Cooley High* was written by Eric Monte. He'd grown up in the Cabrini-Green Housing Projects and graduated from Cooley Vocational. Many of the events in the movie were based on his real-life experiences. Monte was also one of the creators of a successful TV series set in Cabrini-Green called *Good Times.*

Michael Schultz was the director of *Cooley High.* In 1969, at the age of twenty-one, he'd earned a Tony nomination for the Broadway play *Does a Tiger Wear a Necktie?* Schultz had then gone on to direct some television shows and a couple of low-budget feature films.

*Cooley High* opens with a tracking shot of the downtown Chicago skyline, while the Supremes' "Baby Love" provides the background music, the first of many classic cuts that fill the soundtrack. The words "CHICAGO 1964" flash across the screen. The camera then follows an "L" train up to the Near North Side, Cabrini-Green, and Cooley High itself.

Now we see high school senior Richard "Cochise" Morris (Lawrence Hilton-Jacobs) walking through the projects. He's wearing an awards jacket identifying him as a member of the "All City Basketball" team. It's a school day, and Cochise enters one of the townhouses to roust his best friend out of bed. This is Leroy "Preach" Jackson (Glynn Turman). Preach is a glasses-wearing nerd. He's also an underachiever who hasn't been to school all week.

Cochise and Preach arrive at Cooley. But they don't stay long. Along with a couple of other buddies, they cut class, hop on the back end of a passing CTA bus, and head off for some extracurricular fun. The Cooley quartet does some mischief at Lincoln Park Zoo, then returns to the neighborhood to kill more time.

There are some hoops, some dice, some drinking, some fumbling making-out in a stairwell. Cochise learns that he has received his hoped-for college basketball scholarship. Preach pursues Brenda (Cynthia Davis), a "good girl"

*Cooley High—* originally Lane Tech, the building made famous as Cooley High. *Author's collection.*

who wants to reform him. Meanwhile, Mr. Mason (Garrett Morris), a tough-but-sympathetic history teacher, tries to get his students to live up to their potential, or at least make it through graduation.

The cast of *Cooley High* included a number of nonprofessional actors. Two key roles were filled by gangbangers who'd been referred to the producers by the Chicago Police Department. Dozens of Cooley students were also hired as extras. (One of those extras later became one of my teaching colleagues, and on the last day of school, I'd screen her clips to her class.)

The first hour of *Cooley High* is played for laughs. Preach and another pal fake a nosebleed to be excused from class, while Cochise crawls out along the floor. The guys tease a gorilla at the zoo, and the gorilla responds in an appropriate manner. Cochise and Preach pretend to be cops to shake down a couple of hookers for movie money. The owner of the local teen hangout enforces her "no gambling" rule with a meat cleaver.

Then things become serious. Cochise and Preach decide to take a joyride in a Cadillac with a couple of other guys. The Caddy turns out to be stolen. From there, events cascade into a tragic conclusion. Finally—again, like *American Graffiti*—the postscript of *Cooley High* tells us what eventually happened to the characters we've followed for 107 minutes.

*Cooley High* became a major box office hit. Actors Lawrence Hilton-Jacobs, Glynn Turman, and Garret Morris segued into television work. Writer Eric Monte cloned a new TV series from the movie titled *What's Happening!* Michael Schultz continued as a director, with 112 credits at the time of this writing. Cynthia Davis never acted again, and for the past four decades has communicated with the movie's fans strictly through rumor.

## *Continental Divide* (1981)

John Belushi? Romantic comedy? That name and that phrase don't go together—unless you take the time to watch *Continental Divide*.

In 1981 Belushi was enjoying his first successes as a movie headliner. He had been playing boisterous, gonzo roles in epics like *Animal House* and *The Blues Brothers*. Now he was trying something different. *Continental Divide* is a film in the Spencer Tracy-Katharine Hepburn "Opposites Attract" style.

The film opens with an establishing shot of the Chicago lakefront. We move into downtown, to the old *Sun-Times* building on the river off Wabash Avenue. Now we move into the newsroom, where we meet columnist Ernie Souchak (Belushi).

Souchak is a rumpled guy with a sarcastic streak. He's patterned after iconic Chicago columnist Mike Royko, who was then writing for the *Sun-Times*. In real life, Royko had been a friend of the Belushi family for years, so close that John Belushi called him "Uncle Mike."

Everybody in town knows Ernie Souchak—even a couple of muggers, who apologize for robbing him. And what would a Chicago movie be without a crooked politician? In the film, he's an alderman named Yablonowitz (Val Avery). Souchak is out to nail him.

A beating from the alderman's thugs puts Souchak in the hospital. The editor (Allen Goorwitz, also known as Garfield) decides to get his star columnist out of harm's way for a while. He sends Souchak to the Rocky Mountains to track down reclusive ornithologist Nell Porter (Blair Brown).

All this action has taken up fifteen minutes. The great middle of the film is about Souchak's adventures in the Rockies.

Souchak hires a local guide to take him to Nell Porter's cabin while she's off doing some work with bald eagles. When Nell gets back, she meets Ernie. They can't stand each other. Nell isn't happy about having an uninvited reporter invade her privacy. She lets him stay only because the guide has gone. For his part, Ernie doesn't relish being stuck with Nell for two weeks—"I'd like to get this chick in a bowling alley," he mutters.

Ernie perseveres. With some comic missteps, he begins adjusting to his surroundings. Ernie comes to respect Nell's work. Nell comes to respect Ernie's sincere attempts to fit in. And in one of the film's funniest episodes, she unexpectedly discovers that Ernie is also a legend in his own field.

By now we all know what's going to happen to Ernie and Nell's relationship. The way it is handled is funny, and gentle, and believable.

The idyll ends. Ernie goes back to Chicago. Pining for Nell, his columns lose their edge. But Alderman Yablonowitz pulls one trick too many. Ernie gets recharged and has his final showdown with the alderman.

Meanwhile, Nell has arrived in Chicago to give a lecture. Ernie and Nell reconnect, and he takes the opportunity to show her around his city. In the end, their romance is resolved in a way that looks forward to a possible sequel.

*Continental Divide* opened to mixed reviews. Its box office performance was reasonably strong, and that sequel became a possibility. But six months after the premiere, Belushi was dead from a drug overdose.

Blair Brown as Nell perfectly captures the essence of her character, the dedicated, all-business scientist who finds herself unaccountably charmed by the raffish newsman—and she even looks a bit like a young Katie Hepburn.

The supporting players do their jobs well, particularly Carlin Glynn as the editor's down-to-earth wife. Then there is John Belushi.

As an actor, Belushi is no Spencer Tracy. Yet he is surprisingly good. The problem is, he's up against his own persona—he doesn't deliver what we expect from John Belushi. If Richard Dreyfus had been cast as Souchak and had given the same caliber performance, the film would have been better received, and more fondly remembered.

The Chicago filming locations are limited to downtown. As always, it's interesting to see what the city looked like at a particular moment in the past—and to think about how much it has changed. I suspect that most of the Rocky Mountain scenery hasn't changed.

Watching *Continental Divide* thirty years after its release, a critic said that the movie gave him one more reason to wish John Belushi had taken better care of himself. I feel the same way.

# 7.
# THE PASSING PARADE

## PROFESSOR MORIARTY COMES TO CHICAGO

Adam Worth ran a criminal ring in England during the latter part of the nineteenth century. A London detective once called him the "Napoleon of the Criminal World," and Worth is thought to have been the model for Sherlock Holmes's nemesis Professor Moriarty. And though Holmes never had any dealings in Chicago, the real-life Moriarty did.

Born in Germany in 1841, Worth grew up in Massachusetts. He eventually settled in London, posing as an American financier with social connections. During the 1870s he put together an elaborate underworld organization, specializing in high-end burglaries of his unsuspecting society friends. Scotland Yard suspected him but could prove nothing.

Then, in 1876, Worth's brother was arrested on forgery charges and needed bail. At the time a famous Gainsborough painting, *Georgiana, Duchess of Devonshire*, was about to be offered at a London auction. So, one night, Worth simply got a ladder, climbed through a window at the auction house, cut the painting from its frame, and made off with it.

As it turned out, the charges against little brother were dropped. Rather than fence the stolen painting, Worth decided to keep it.

*Georgiana* became Worth's constant companion. He usually kept it in the false bottom of a suitcase as he traveled. At some point he smuggled the painting out of England and put it in storage in the United States. That's

Adam Worth, the model for Professor Moriarty. *From* Leslie's Monthly Magazine, *June 1905.*

where *Georgiana* was in 1893, when Belgian authorities convicted Worth of a string of robberies and sent him to prison.

By 1899 Worth was again free. His crime ring was in shambles, and his fortune was gone. Using the Pinkerton Detective Agency as a go-between, he began negotiating a "no-questions-asked" return of *Georgiana* to the auction house. After nearly two years of haggling, a price of $25,000 was agreed on. The transfer was to be made at Pinkerton's headquarters city, Chicago.

Morland Agnew of the auction house came over from London with his wife, arriving in Chicago on March 27, 1901. They were met at the train station by William Pinkerton of the detective agency. Pinkerton assured the Agnews that things were moving forward according to plan and offered to take the visitors on a tour of the city. The Agnews declined. Exhausted and anxious, the couple checked into the Auditorium Hotel for a good night's sleep.

At 9:30 the next morning, Morland Agnew and Pinkerton made their way to the First National Bank to cash a bank draft for the ransom. When the cashier examined the size of the draft, he warned Agnew, "That's a lot of money to carry around Chicago!" Agnew simply nodded and gestured toward Pinkerton, who was standing just behind him. Everyone in Chicago knew William Pinkerton. "Oh, I guess you'll be all right then," the cashier said.

As instructed, the money was made up of used bills. Agnew carried it to Pinkerton's office, where the two men sorted it out. Then they returned to the hotel. The painting was to be delivered there at 1:00 p.m.

Mrs. Agnew had been left alone at the hotel while her husband and Pinkerton assembled the ransom. By then the tension was getting to her, and she was a nervous wreck. As the hours slowly passed, Agnew and Pinkerton also became apprehensive. *Was Worth going to carry out his part of the bargain?*

At precisely 1:00 p.m., a messenger arrived at the Agnews' hotel room, carrying a parcel wrapped in brown paper. After Morland Agnew identified himself and handed over the money, the messenger surrendered the parcel. Inside it was the long-lost *Georgiana*.

Within hours the Agnews were on the train to New York, and from there, the ship to England. Not until the painting was safely back in London was the news released to the public. Then the Chicago papers ran the story on the front page for a week.

Adam Worth, in disguise, had been the messenger returning the painting. Less than a year after collecting the ransom, he was dead of natural causes. But in a twist worthy of Conan Doyle himself, the son of the real-life Moriarty refused to take over the family business. Instead, he found a new career—as a Pinkerton detective.

# Kiss of Fire

Jack Eigen made his name on the radio during the 1940s with celebrity interviews streamed from the Copacabana nightclub in New York. He later claimed to have invented the talk radio format. While that might be stretching things, Eigen could be considered the first "radio personality." With a self-regard that earned him the nickname "Jack Ego," he put himself on an equal footing with his guests.

And it worked. By 1948 his show was one of the most popular on radio. He played himself in a couple of movies. The Marlin sisters even celebrated him with a record titled "The Jack Eigen Polka."

WMAQ lured Eigen to Chicago in 1951 to host a nightclub interview show from the Chez Paree. In New York he had found time to broadcast a fifteen-minute television program. Once he established himself in Chicago, Eigen again branched out, signing on to do a late-night show over WBKB-TV, the local ABC affiliate.

Early-day television was usually free-flowing, and Eigen liked it that way. His guest on the February 15, 1954 telecast was Cleo Moore. A twenty-nine-year-old native of Louisiana, Moore was an actress who was more decorative than talented. She was in Chicago to promote her latest epic, *Bait*.

It was the day after Saint Valentine's Day. The conversation inevitably turned to romance—and kissing. Some sources say that Eigen asked Moore to "show me how they do it in Hollywood." Others say that Eigen suggested, "Let's go for the record!" Whatever he said, they started to kiss.

By today's standards, the kiss was pretty tame. Eigen and Moore were seated in separate chairs. They kept their hands inactive. They kept their mouths closed.

What wasn't tame was the length of the kiss. Eigen and Moore remained in osculation for two minutes—or three minutes, or five minutes, again, depending on your source. Yet another report states that the duo came up for air only because it was time for a commercial. When they did break, Eigen compared Moore's kissing skill to that of his wife.

Public response was immediate. Phone calls from irate viewers poured in. The station's regular switchboard was closed, so some callers settled for complaining to the all-night traffic department. Others tracked down station employees at their homes. The vast majority of the complaints were from women.

WBKB's response was also immediate. The next morning, the station vice-president sent a telegram to Eigen. It read: "Regret to inform you that due to extreme poor taste exhibited in telecast of Monday night in putting on a kissing exhibition that under no circumstances can be considered acceptable television fare in the homes of our viewers, we must terminate your services with the program of Monday, Feb 15th."

Eigen was out of a television job, but unapologetic. "I have no guilty conscience," he told the *Tribune*. "I have been happily married for eighteen years, and my wife knew what I had planned for the program. If she had any thought that there was anything unladylike or rude in it, she would have told me."

*Sun-Times* columnist Irv Kupcinet labeled the Eigen-Moore incident "The Kiss of Fire." The story was widely reported in the national press. *Newsweek* ran a picture of the pair doing an ex post facto bit of grooming. That was instructive. Since a photographer had been on hand to document the action, the kiss seemed to be nothing more than a publicity stunt—which backfired.

In the aftermath, Moore insisted that the kiss was "certainly not meant to be offensive" and said, "I wouldn't want anyone to lose his job." She mused that "people don't ask me for my autograph anymore." Still, her career remained on its trajectory, with more movies after *Bait* and more TV appearances. She even staged another marathon kiss on a New Orleans radio show. Cleo Moore eventually married a real estate tycoon, retired from films, and became a Los Angeles socialite.

The WBKB firing proved to only be a bump in Jack Eigen's career. He remained a presence in Chicago radio for decades and later returned to TV to host a succession of local shows—though all of them were short-lived. In 1971 he left Chicago and moved to Florida. He was still doing a radio show there when he died in 1983.

# THE ORIGINAL WALKING MAN

Most Chicagoans know about the Walking Man—the tall guy with the long hair and mustache who silently stalks the downtown streets. His reappearance each spring is usually good for a few lines in the papers or a few thousand tweets on the net.

Over 150 years ago, the city greeted another walking man. His arrival made national news. His name was Edward Payson Weston.

Born in Rhode Island in 1839, Weston spent his teens roaming around the country. He worked as a reporter and as a circus roustabout, traveled with a singing troupe, and failed at a number of other jobs. Politics finally found him his life's work, though not in the customary manner.

Over dinner one night in 1860, Weston and a friend were talking about the upcoming presidential election. Weston was sure Abraham Lincoln had no chance of being elected and said that he would walk from Boston to Washington, D.C., to attend the inauguration if Lincoln won. When Lincoln did win, Weston walked the five-hundred-mile distance in ten days. It was a charming story for a country that was about to be torn apart by a civil war, and Weston got his first taste of fame.

Weston's war service as a Union dispatch runner was short and unremarkable. By 1867 he was deeply in debt when he met a promoter named George Goodwin. Remembering Weston's inauguration trek, Goodwin bet fellow businessman T.F. Wilcox $10,000 that Weston could walk the 1,226 miles from Portland, Maine, to Chicago in thirty days.

Weston eagerly agreed to the plan. His share of the possible winnings would be $4,000. He would also receive a $6,000 bonus if he walked 100 miles in a single day.

Weston stepped off from Portland at noon on October 29, 1867. He covered the first 105 miles to Boston in two days without incident. Then, as he moved through New England, crowds began to gather. In anticipation of the large turnout, Weston carried with him a supply of studio portraits, which he sold for twenty-five cents each.

The press picked up the story and ran with it. *Harper's Weekly* magazine and most of the newspapers were supportive, considering Weston's "pedestrianism" an athletic endeavor. Still, some thought him nothing more than a publicity seeker. There were also reports of counterfeit Westons strolling through towns and grabbing shares of his glory.

Weston walked on. In Providence three young women rushed out of the crowd to give him a wreath and kiss him. In Buffalo he had dinner with ex-

Edward Payson Weston, a professional pedestrian. *Author's collection.*

president Fillmore. In Fremont, Ohio, local police saved him from thugs who'd been hired to delay his progress. In South Bend enthusiastic crowds pushed into his hotel to get a look at him while he tried to sleep.

During his journey, Weston made several attempts to win the bonus for walking one hundred miles in a day. Each time he came up short. One newspaper noted that many of Weston's friends had been betting against this and suggested Weston was in on the fix. Nothing was ever proven.

Fearing last-minute sabotage, Weston arranged for an armed escort on the final leg of his journey. He arrived at the village of Hyde Park on the evening of the twenty-ninth day of his journey. The next morning he began his final walk into Chicago.

Thousands of spectators lined Wabash Avenue as Weston made his victory lap on November 28—Thanksgiving Day. They waved American flags and cheered themselves hoarse. As the conquering hero approached the Sherman House Hotel, the crush was so thick that police had to clear the way. At the hotel he gave a short speech to his admirers before retiring. The next few days saw a series of public exhibitions and testimonial dinners before "Weston fever" gradually subsided.

Edward Payson Weston parlayed his 1867 Chicago trek into a fifty-year career as a professional "pedestrian." He performed all over America and Europe, and was respected enough to be featured in a tobacco card series of famous athletes. In 1927 the man who'd walked from New York to San Francisco in one hundred days suffered the indignity of being hit by a taxi while crossing the street. He never fully recovered, and died in 1929.

# THE OTHER CHICAGO FIRE

The Great Chicago Fire of 1871 began on the evening of October 8, when a barn on DeKoven Street caught fire. Pushed on by strong southwest winds, the flames roared into the business district, jumped the river, and swept through the North Side before burning out a day later near Fullerton Avenue. More than seventeen thousand buildings were destroyed in an area covering 2,100 acres. About three hundred people were killed.

The 1871 fire was notorious enough to earn a star on Chicago's official flag. Yet another, smaller fire a few years later also had a lasting impact on the city's history.

The "other" Chicago fire began on the afternoon of July 14, 1874. Around 4:30 p.m., the city fire department received an alarm from a box at Clark and Twelfth Streets. Arriving at the scene shortly afterward, the firefighters realized the blaze was already burning out of control. Chicago had been enduring hot, dry, and windy weather for some days—just like in October 1871.

The fire marshal called out every available man and piece of equipment. This area directly south of downtown, called Little Cheyenne, had been

After the Fire of 1874, a real "fire sale." *From the* Chicago Tribune, *July 19, 1874.*

untouched by the 1871 fire. The blocks were crammed tight with wooden shacks that fed the flames. The fire continued moving north. All attempts to contain it failed.

Meanwhile, people downtown could see the approaching flames. They could feel the heat. Once again, they began packing their belongings onto wagons and pulling out.

Night fell, and the fire had reached as far north as Van Buren Street. Then the firefighters caught a break. The wind shifted, turning the flames toward the east. And at Van Buren Street, the fire came up against the solidly built, flame-resistant brick structures that had gone up in the aftermath of the 1871 blaze. By midnight the new fire had burned itself out along the lakefront.

The 1874 fire had destroyed 812 structures in an area comprising forty-seven acres. Twenty people had died. The total property damage was pegged to cost $1,067,260—about $22,000,000 today. Soon afterward, Chicago newspapers began referring to this blaze as "the little big fire."

Unlike the Great Fire of 1871, the origin of the 1874 fire has never been determined. The most common story is that it started in a barn next to an oil works on Clark Street. Nathan Isaacson, the owner of the barn, was arrested on a charge of arson. He was later acquitted in court, and most historians conclude that he was simply a victim of antisemitic hysteria.

The 1871 fire had spurred the city council into enacting fire limits. The idea was to protect the central business district from another catastrophe. No new wood buildings would be permitted in the area bounded by the Chicago River, Halsted Street, Twenty-Second Street and Lake Michigan—though existing wood buildings would be allowed to remain.

*Problem solved?* Not quite. As one historian put it, "Then caution gave way to indiscretion." A proposal to extend the fire limits to include the entire city was defeated. The council also began allowing temporary wood structures within the boundaries until permanent brick or stone structures could be erected. Nothing was said about how long those "temporary" buildings might stay in place.

But the second big fire in less than three years forced some real action. Disgusted with the dithering of Chicago politicians, the eastern insurance companies threatened to stop writing fire policies in the city. Meanwhile, a group of concerned residents formed the Citizens' Association of Chicago to put pressure on officials. The association brought in General Alexander Shaler, a war hero and the head of the New York City Fire Department, to study local conditions and make recommendations for improvement.

The 1874 fire cleared out many of the grandfathered wood buildings just south of downtown. Now the fire limits were extended to cover the entire city. The fire department was reorganized. An executive department to inspect buildings was established. The city's single pumping station was joined by five new ones. Other safety laws were enacted, including a requirement that nonresidential buildings were to have outdoor metal fire escapes. These are some of the lasting legacies of Chicago's forgotten fire.

# THE ANNIE OAKLEY COCAINE CASE

During the 1880s and 1890s, Annie Oakley was the star attraction of Buffalo Bill Cody's Wild West Show. She was a pretty young lady, a sharpshooter who could hit a dime tossed in the air thirty feet away or split a playing card edge-on. Once she shot the ash off a burning cigarette held in the mouth of the German emperor. "Little Miss Sure Shot" was known and loved by millions of fans on three continents.

Then, in the summer of 1903, came the shocking news: Annie Oakley was in jail in Chicago.

The August 11 issue of the *Chicago American* told the story. A scruffy-looking woman had been arrested for stealing the pants of a man who'd befriended her. While in custody, she had admitted that she was Annie Oakley. She had stolen the pants to support her cocaine habit.

"I plead guilty, your honor, but I hope you will have pity on me," the woman told the judge when she was arraigned at the Harrison Street Police Court. "An uncontrollable appetite for drugs has brought me here. I began the use of it years ago to steady me under the strain of the show life I was leading, and now, it has lost me everything. Please give me a chance to pull myself together."

The judge was unmoved. He imposed a fine of forty-five dollars on the woman, committing her to the Bridewell Prison Farm until it was paid. "A good, long stay [there] will do you good," he said.

Annie Oakley herself. *From* Buffalo
Bill's Wild West and Congress of
Rough Riders of the World *(1893).*

"The striking beauty of the woman whom the crowds at the World's Fair
admired is now entirely gone," the newspaper report went on. "Although she
is but twenty-eight years old, she looks almost forty. Hers, in fact, is one of
the extreme cases which have come up in the Harrison Street Police Court."

The downfall of a celebrity has always been an enticing story. It somehow
demonstrates that they are no better than we are. Instead of having
sympathy for them, we gloat. The Germans call this all-too-human reaction
*schadenfreude*—taking pleasure in the misfortune of others.

The tale of Annie Oakley's sad fate was soon picked up by the wire
services. From Chicago, the saga spread across the country. It was read with
particular interest by Mrs. Frank Butler of Nutley, New Jersey. She was the
*real* Annie Oakley.

Oakley immediately started writing to newspapers, exposing the impostor.
After investigating the matter, the Publishers Press wire service issued a
retraction. The woman in Chicago turned out to be Maude Fontanella.

Fontanella was a small-time vaudeville performer who had once appeared
in a burlesque Wild West show as "Any Oakley." Probably seeking better

treatment while in jail, she had "accidentally" told a matron that she was the noted sharpshooter. The matron, in turn, had tipped off local reporters. The reporter from the *American* had actually seen Annie Oakley perform at the World's Fair years before, but Fontanella had fooled him as well.

The newspapers began printing their own retractions. Apologies poured in to Oakley. That was not good enough for her. She decided to take legal action. Perhaps having to pay out money would make the press more careful in their reporting. She felt that she was being reasonable in taking this approach to the insult. "In the South they simply kill the man who slanders the good name of a woman," she told a reporter.

Over the next seven years, Oakley brought suit against fifty-five newspapers. She traveled from city to city to personally testify in court. William Randolph Hearst, whose *American* had printed the initial story, hired a detective to look for any dirt that might be used against Oakley. Nothing was found.

In the end, Annie Oakley won judgments or settlements from all but one of the fifty-five newspapers. The total awards came to $625,000—the equivalent of $25 million today. Adding up her legal fees, travel expenses, and missed income, it is possible Oakley had actually lost money in her pursuit of justice. But her reputation had been restored, and the case is considered a landmark in celebrity libel law.

# JUDY'S JOLLY JAUNT

Question: How does an elephant travel? Answer: Any way he wants to.

In this case, the elephant was a she. Her name was Judy, she was Asian, and in the summer of 1943, she was thirty-five years old. She lived at Brookfield Zoo.

Over in the city, Lincoln Park Zoo's prize pachyderm Deed-a-Day had just died. Lincoln Park needed a new elephant. Brookfield agreed to sell them Judy for $2,500. That was a cut-rate price for an elephant in the prime of her life, and Lincoln Park officials were pleased with the deal.

The purchase price, however, did not include shipping. So, on the morning of July 2, two Lincoln Park elephant handlers drove out to Brookfield to collect their new elephant. The plan was to transport Judy by truck. It was a routine assignment.

Elephants are smart. Judy had been a resident at Brookfield for years and enjoyed suburban life. Perhaps she figured out that the two smiling men in the Lincoln Park Zoo dusters wanted to hustle her off to the bustling metropolis. Nobody had consulted her about relocating. She refused to get into the truck.

The handlers thought maybe familiar faces would help get Judy moving. Now the Brookfield elephant handlers took over from their Lincoln Park colleagues. They tried soothing words, they tried threats, they tried loading hay into the truck ahead of Judy—but without success. Judy wouldn't budge.

Other zookeepers came forward. Twenty different people took turns attempting to get Judy to cooperate. In the process, the 7,200-pound elephant became rambunctious and wrecked the Lincoln Park truck.

Hours passed. One of the Lincoln Park handlers finally phoned his boss to advise him that they were having a "little difficulty" with Judy. The Lincoln Park director listened to the report and made an executive decision: the reluctant elephant would have to be moved the old-fashioned way. "Let her walk," he ordered.

In 1943 the most direct way to get from Brookfield Zoo to Lincoln Park Zoo was straight up Ogden Avenue. That idea was discarded because of the heavy traffic on Ogden. A more circuitous—but more sedate—route was chosen instead.

At 7:00 p.m., Judy left Brookfield Zoo and began walking north on First Avenue. Her party included the four handlers from the two zoos, a motorcycle police escort, three support trucks, and twenty armed attendants. Ahead of them was eighteen miles of suburb and city.

The caravan traveled up First Avenue to Maywood. They turned right at Washington Boulevard and moved east into River Forest. At Des Plaines Avenue in Forest Park, they stopped at a gas station so Judy could get some water. Then they were moving again, through Oak Park and into Chicago.

There had been no public announcement of Judy's trek. Eight decades ago, there was no social media. Yet somehow, the news had gotten out. Just imagine a guy in Maywood phoning a friend on the West Side of Chicago to say, "Hey, there's an elephant walking down the middle of Washington Boulevard!" In any event, thousands of people turned up to watch the unplanned parade. The *Tribune* reported that the fans gathered along Judy's route made it "a veritable victory march."

By 10:00 p.m. Judy and her party had reached Garfield Park. They rested there for two hours while Judy snacked on some hay. At midnight, as they set off again, they were onto the home stretch. Traffic was thinning when they swung onto Ogden Avenue for the final few miles. At 2:15 a.m. on July

3, Judy arrived at her new home. Once she was settled into her quarters, she quickly went to sleep.

Judy's road trip had taken a little over seven hours. In the course of her eighteen-mile journey, she had lost one hundred pounds. One of the attendants who'd walked along with her had his feet swell so badly that he couldn't get back into his shoes for two days.

The Great Elephant Walk took place in the middle of World War II and gave Chicagoans a few chuckles in the middle of a grim time. Suburbanite Judy soon adapted to city life. She remained one of the star attractions at Lincoln Park Zoo until her death in 1971.

# THE CHICAGO GRAND PRIX OF 1895

In 1895 the automobile was a novelty. There wasn't even agreement on what to call the new vehicle—horseless carriage, motocycle, motor wagon, and road machine were some of the names used. The general public considered it a toy for rich eccentrics.

That June the world's first auto race was run in France. On July 9, the *Chicago Times-Herald* announced it was following the French lead. The paper would stage the first American auto race, with a $5,000 prize fund. The winner would receive $2,000. The date set was November 2.

The race was widely publicized throughout the country. Understandably, the other Chicago papers ignored it. The *Tribune* took delight in obliquely tweaking its rival, with stories highlighting the noise and unreliability of the devil wagon.

Meanwhile, the planned race was running into complications. The original course was supposed to run from Chicago to Milwaukee and back. But because rural roads were nothing more than dirt paths, the northern turnaround was initially cut back to Waukegan. The final course was set over a route from Jackson Park in Chicago to Evanston and back, a round trip of fifty-four miles.

The *Times-Herald* had hoped to attract eighty autos. When entries were slow in coming in, the paper pushed race day back four weeks to November 28, Thanksgiving Day.

By mid-November only eleven cars had arrived in town. Then the weather turned bad. Thanksgiving morning found the city blanketed with six inches of snow. Five of the eleven entries dropped out.

Two models of 1895 "motocycles." *From the* International Gazette, *November 30, 1895.*

But snow or not, a crowd of two thousand people gathered around the starting point on Midway Plaisance at Stony Island Avenue to watch the start of the great race. Atop the nearby Illinois Central Overpass, the umpire gave the signal. And at 8:55 a.m., the six cars roared west down the Midway at a breakneck speed of twelve miles per hour.

The race route headed west through Washington Park to Michigan Avenue, then north on Michigan Avenue to downtown. From there, it followed Lake Shore Drive and Sheridan Road into Evanston, to a turnaround near the Grosse Point Light House. Coming back south, the course ran through Evanston and onto Chicago's Clark Street, continuing down Clark Street as far as Lawrence Avenue. The route then followed a circuitous path over several streets, moving through Humboldt, Garfield, and Douglas Parks. The final stretch ran south on Western Boulevard to Garfield Boulevard, then back east to the finish line at Jackson Park.

The *Times-Herald* had provided direction markers along the route to guide the cars, and policemen on horseback rode ahead to clear the way. The paper also printed a tentative schedule for spectators. The cars were expected to enter Lincoln Park at 10:30 a.m., reach the Evanston turnaround at noon, Milwaukee-Belmont at 2:00 p.m., Western-Garfield at 4:00 p.m. and, finally, the Jackson Park finish line at 4:30 p.m. People who were interested in watching the cars were advised to be situated along the route ahead of the schedule, since "it is quite likely that some of the machines will make better time than this."

However, the weather continued to play havoc with the primitive, open vehicles. The De La Vergne Refrigerating Machine was the first to drop out after seven miles. The electric-powered Sturges lasted twelve miles. By the early afternoon, when the cars turned around to head back south, only three were still running.

Frank Duryea's car had taken the lead early in the race. As the day moved on, drifting snow covered some of the direction markers. Duryea missed the turn at Lawrence Avenue and continued on down Clark Street. He finally got back on course, only to be stopped at a railroad crossing as a freight train slowly rumbled through.

At 7:18 p.m. Duryea finally crept through the darkness to the Jackson Park finish line. Only then did he discover his was the first car to complete the race. A little over an hour later, a second car arrived. The third survivor straggled in around midnight.

Duryea had not followed the official race course. But then, neither had the other two finishers. Still, the *Times-Herald* was satisfied, and it distributed cash awards in nine categories, with Frank Duryea claiming the $2,000 grand prize. Today he is recognized as the winner of America's first auto race.

# DEATH VALLEY SCOTTY'S WILD RIDE

Walter E. Scott (1872–1954) was famous for being famous. Known to the world as Death Valley Scotty, he was a relentless self-promoter. For forty years he conned the gullible with tales of hidden desert gold mines. And Chicago played a singular role in establishing his legend.

In 1905 Scott was reckoned to be a wealthy but eccentric miner. On July 8 he walked into the Los Angeles office of John Byrne, the Santa Fe Railroad's assistant traffic manager. "I've been thinking some of taking a train over your road to Chicago," Scott told Byrne. "I want you to put me in there in forty-six hours."

No train had ever made the 2,265-mile Los Angeles–Chicago run in less than fifty-one hours. Byrne did some calculating and said that the railroad could meet Scott's schedule. The price for the chartered train would be

$5,500—about $160,000 today. With that, Scott pulled out a wad of $100 bills and paid the fare. Byrne said the train would be ready the next day.

That's the way the story is usually told. Scott never did say why he wanted to get to Chicago so fast. What is known is that the Santa Fe Railroad was then in cut-throat competition with two other roads—and it was losing. Setting a new speed record would be great publicity. Most likely, Byrne and Scott had been cooking up the plan for some time.

At 1:03 p.m. on July 9, a crowd of one thousand people watched the three-car Scott Special steam out of Santa Fe's La Grande Station. An enhanced crew of fifteen men was on board. The passengers were Scott; his wife, Ella; a Santa Fe publicity man; a newspaper reporter; and a stray yellow dog.

The Los Angeles dispatcher telegraphed ahead to clear the track for the special trip. Arrangements were made to have relief engines and engineers ready at intervals of approximately 120 miles. An entire change over to a fresh machine and a fresh man took only about three minutes.

The trip went smoothly. The one mishap occurred in Kansas when a cylinder blew on the engine. After a slight delay for this unexpected change over, the train was moving again. By the time it crossed the Mississippi River into Illinois, it was an hour ahead of schedule. Over one three-mile stretch, the special sustained a reported speed of 106 miles per hour, faster than any steam-driven train had ever traveled.

All throughout the journey, the onboard reporter telegraphed dispatches on the train's progress. Newspapers throughout the country ran the story. Heavy gambling was booked on whether or not Scott's train would beat the forty-six-hour mark.

Chicago eagerly awaited the special's arrival. Rumor said that Scott never tipped less than $10, and he was known to pass out $100 bills if the mood struck him. Cornelius Shea, the president of the local teamsters' union, was especially interested in meeting the "millionaire miner." "He does not know what to do with his money," Shea told a reporter. "I know what to do with a bunch of it if he will give it to me."

The Scott Special chugged into Dearborn Street Station at 11:57 a.m. local time on July 11, 1905, forty-four hours and fifty-four minutes after its departure from Los Angeles. A cheer went up from the thousands of people who were present as Scott stepped off the train. One woman rushed forward and kissed him. "Ladies and gentleman," Scott shouted to the crowd. "I'm glad to see you—" but the rest of his words were drowned out by more cheers. Then Scott, his wife, and the yellow dog were off to the Great Northern Hotel.

THE RECEPTION COMMITTEE WAITING TO GREET MR. SCOTT OF CALIFORNIA.

Part of the crowd that awaited the arrival of Death Valley Scotty's train in Chicago. *From the* Chicago Tribune, *July 13, 1905.*

Over the next two days, reports trickled out that the "free-spending" Scott was hanging onto his supposed fortune. Salesmen, inventors, investment brokers, and everyday panhandlers were turned away from his suite empty-handed. The largest amount he parted with was a thirty-cent tip to the room service waiter.

Then, on July 13, Scott was off to New York on "new business." He was accompanied by the yellow dog. Mrs. Scott joined them several days later.

Today we know that Walter Scott's gold mine boasts were nothing more than desert hot air. But that 1905 record train run was the one time he was as good as his word.

## WORLD'S PARLIAMENT OF RELIGIONS

In 1890, planning was underway for the World's Columbian Exposition, the giant fair that was to be held in Chicago in 1893. People would be coming to the city from all parts of the globe. To take advantage of this gathering, fair officials decided to organize meetings where ideas on different issues could be shared. Separate conventions would discuss education, labor, moral and social reform, medicine, literature, and women's progress, among other topics.

But the most ambitious program came from the fair's Religion Department. First a series of separate conclaves were to be scheduled for more than forty mostly Protestant denominations. And that was only the beginning. The climax would be the World's Parliament of Religions.

The United States was a Protestant country in 1893. The number of American Catholics was growing, but it was still small. The only non-Christians most Americans had contact with were Jews, who made up about 2 percent of the nation's population. Bringing together representatives of major world religions in one place was mind boggling. Nothing like that had ever been done.

It was time for all faiths to concentrate on what they had in common, rather than what divided them. As Judge Charles C. Bonney of the Religion Department said, the parliament's purpose was "to unite all religion against all irreligion, make the Golden Rule the basis of this union, and present to the world…the substantial unity of many religions in the good deeds of the religious life."

Three thousand detailed invitations to the World's Parliament of Religions were sent to religious leaders around the world. As expected, a few of them were opposed to the idea—the Anglican archbishop of Canterbury refused to attend, declaring that all religions were not equal. The Ottoman sultan declined to send a representative for similar reasons. However, most of the response was positive.

Like the other conventions, the Parliament of Religions was scheduled to meet in Columbus Hall. The building on Michigan Avenue at Adams Street was set to become the new home of the Art Institute of Chicago once the fair closed. The fair directors had paid one-third of its construction costs in return for use of the premises.

Four thousand people turned out to watch the parliament's opening ceremonies on the morning of September 11, 1893. At 10:00 a.m., a dozen representatives from ten different faiths marched in, hand in hand. The senior Catholic prelate of the United States, James Cardinal Gibbons, led the gathering in the Lord's Prayer. Then each of the dozen representatives gave a short speech.

The parliament met for seventeen days. Again, this was the United States in 1893, so most of the proceedings reflected the then-current demographic—152 of the 194 of the papers delivered over the seventeen days were from English-speaking Christians. The only Muslim in attendance was a Massachusetts journalist who'd converted to Islam.

Still, there were representatives of Judaism and Buddhism and Taoism and Confucianism and other faiths. One of the delegates was Swami Vivekananda from India. Most people in the Western hemisphere had no experience with Hinduism in 1893, and the swami's three eloquent speeches on tolerance received much favorable publicity.

The parliament also took the extraordinary step of inviting two apostles of "irreligion" to attend—Thomas Huxley and Herbert Spencer. The two English biologists had done a lot to promote Darwin's theory of evolution and were looked on with suspicion by religious leaders. Unfortunately, neither man could attend, though Spencer did have his paper read to a less-than-enthusiastic audience.

As with any group of humans, different delegates to the parliament had different agendas. Some of them wished to learn about other beliefs. Some wished to correct misconceptions about their particular faith. Some wished to find a common ground among differing faiths. And some frankly wished to highlight the superiority of their own religion.

In the end, those motivations didn't matter. When the parliament closed on September 27, it was counted as a success. The first steps had been taken at building an interfaith dialogue.

In 1993 the centennial of the World's Parliament of Religions was celebrated with a new convention at Chicago's Palmer House. Since then, interfaith meetings under this title have become regular events.

# ABOUT THE AUTHOR

John R. Schmidt is a fifth-generation Chicagoan. He earned his PhD in history at the University of Chicago and has taught at all levels, from kindergarten through college, including over thirty years in the Chicago Public School System. He has published over four hundred articles in magazines, newspapers, encyclopedias, and anthologies. This is his sixth book.